THE BATTLING
UNBELIEF

STUDY GUIDE

by DESIRING GOD

MULTNOMAH
BOOKS

THE BATTLING UNBELIEF STUDY GUIDE

published by Multnomah Books

A division of Random House Inc.

© 2006 by Desiring God Ministries

International Standard Book Number: 978-1-59052-920-1

Cover design by The DesignWorks Group

Interior typesest by Katherine Lloyd, The DESK, Sisters, Oregon

Unless otherwise indicated, Scripture quotations are from:

The Holy Bible, *English Standard Version*

© 2001 by Crossway Bibles, a division of Good News Publishers.

Used by permission. All rights reserved.

Multnomah is a trademark of Multnomah Books

and is registered in the U.S. Patent and Trademark Office.

The colophon is a trademark of Multnomah Books

For information:

Multnomah Books

12265 Oracle Boulevard, Suite 200

Colorado Springs, CO 80921

07 08 09 10—10 9 8 7 6 5 4 3

TABLE OF CONTENTS

INTRODUCTION
TO THIS STUDY GUIDE

War. Our world today is familiar with war. Conflicts rage around the world. Nations rise up against other nations. Ethnic groups seek to systematically exterminate other ethnic groups. Sometimes the warfare even finds its way to our own city streets. But the greatest battle in the world is not taking place between foreign governments or terrorist networks or rival gangs. It is taking place over human souls and within human hearts. As the apostle Paul says in Ephesians 6:12, "For we do not wrestle against flesh and blood, but against the rulers, against the authorities, against the cosmic powers over this present darkness, against the spiritual forces of evil in the heavenly places."[1]

Followers of Jesus are not free from this battle. In fact, we know it better than anyone else. As the apostle Peter says, "Beloved, I urge you as sojourners and exiles to abstain from the passions of the flesh, which wage war against your soul" (1 Peter 2:11). This is the battle we find ourselves in: the desires of the flesh versus the desires of the Spirit; the powers of this present evil age versus the power of the resurrection; the lies of the evil one versus the truth of the gospel.

The aim of this study guide is to aid you in this battle. It is our conviction that beneath every sin lies the same root: unbelief.

Therefore, the key to defeating anxiety and covetousness and lust and bitterness and impatience and pride and depression and greed and a thousand other sins is to sever the root of unbelief. And the way to sever this root is to live by faith in future grace. Our prayer is that this study guide and DVD would be used by God to liberate thousands from the deceitful and fleeting pleasures of sin by pointing to the superior satisfaction of knowing Jesus Christ, all to the glory of God.

This study guide is designed to be used in a twelve-session[2] guided group study that focuses on the *Battling Unbelief* DVD Set.[3] After an introductory lesson, each subsequent lesson examines one thirty minute session from *Battling Unbelief*. You, the learner, are encouraged to prepare for the viewing of each session by reading and reflecting upon Scripture, by considering key quotations, and by asking yourself penetrating questions. Your preparatory work for each lesson is marked with the heading "Before You Watch the DVD, Study and Prepare" in Lessons 2–11.

The workload is conveniently divided into five daily (and manageable) assignments. There is also a section suggesting further study. This work is to be completed individually, before the group convenes to view the DVD and discuss the material.

> Throughout this study guide, paragraphs printed in a shaded box (like this one) are excerpts from a book written by John Piper, or excerpts taken from the Desiring God website (www.desiringgod.org). They are included to supplement the study questions and to summarize key or provocative points.

The next section in Lessons 2–9, entitled "While You Watch the DVD, Take Notes," is to be completed as the DVD is playing. You are encouraged to engage with the DVD by filling in the appropriate blanks and writing down other notes that will aid you in the group discussion.

The third section in these weekly lessons is "After You Watch the DVD, Discuss What You've Learned." Three discussion questions are provided to guide and focus the conversation. You may record, in the spaces provided here, notes that will help you contribute to the conversation. Or, you may use this space to record things from the discussion that you want to remember.

The final section is an application section: "After You Discuss, Make Application." You will be challenged to record a "take-away point" and to engage in a certain activity that is a fitting response to the content presented in the lesson.

Group leaders will want to find the *Leader's Guide*, included at the end of this study guide, immediately.

As we've said, life transformation will only occur by the grace of God. Therefore, we highly encourage you to pray throughout the learning process. Pray that God would open your mind to see wonderful things in his Word. Pray that he would grant you the insight, concentration, and attention you need in order to benefit from this resource. Pray that God would cause you to rejoice in the truth. And pray that the discussion in your group would be mutually encouraging and edifying. We've included specific objectives at the beginning of each lesson. These objectives won't be realized without the gracious work of God through prayer.

INTRODUCTION TO
BATTLING UNBELIEF

[handwritten notes, left margin:] Explain study guide – no answers in back to questions an most important Lessons 1 & 12 one different – no DVD, Get price to order more

[handwritten notes, right margin:] Explain study guide Encourage to show up early Start right at 6:30 with 10-20 mts singing 60 mm Lesson 10-20 min praying

LESSON OBJECTIVES

It is our prayer that after you have finished this lesson…

• You will get a feel for how you and others in your group approach the Christian life.

• Your curiosity would be roused, and questions would begin to come to mind.

• You will be eager to learn more about how you can live your life by faith in future grace.

ABOUT YOURSELF

1. What is your name?
2. Tell the group something about yourself that they probably don't already know. *[handwritten:]* – unmet desire for relationships but not good at fostering them
3. Describe your relationship with Jesus.

A PREVIEW OF *BATTLING UNBELIEF*

LESSON
1

1. In your own words, describe your battle against unbelief. How does this battle unfold? What weapons do you have in this battle? Describe any strategies that you use to overcome sin in your life. What motivates you to make war on sin?

2. Think about the phrase "Living by Faith in Future Grace." What do you think this phrase means?

A PASSION FOR GOD'S GLORY AND YOUR JOY

A Companion Study to *Battling Unbelief*, Session 1

LESSON OBJECTIVES

It is our prayer that after you have finished this lesson…

- A passion for the glory of God will be awakened in your soul.

- You will begin to think about how your joy relates to the glory of God.

- You will understand how to approach God in such a way that he always gets the glory.

Before You Watch the DVD, Study and Prepare

DAY 1—SPREADING A PASSION

LESSON 2

DAY 1

Question 1*: When you hear the phrase "the glory of God," what do you think of? How does the glory of God relate to you?[4] Refers to his perfection, purity, sum of all his attributes. We were made in his image so we possess the attributes, just not in perfection. It should bring us comfort because our God is glorious.

The following is John Piper's mission statement:

> I exist to spread a passion for the supremacy of God in all things for the joy of all peoples through Jesus Christ.

Question 2: Each word in this mission statement is carefully chosen. In your own words, describe the significance of the following words. Why do you think each word was chosen instead of other alternatives?

    a. Passion - instead of love, indicates wholehearted driving love

    b. Supremacy - instead of greatness; there is none greater

    c. Joy - instead of happiness, not a fleeting feeling, deeper-rooted;

    d. All peoples -

DAY 2—WHAT GOD IS PASSIONATE ABOUT

Question 3: One of the most important questions in the world is, "What is God passionate about?" How would you answer this question? What do you think God is *most* passionate about? Cite any Bible verses that come to mind.

Us - John 3:16 - For God so loved the world
Psalm 23 ... surely goodness & love will follow us
Psalm 118 - Give thanks to the Lord, for he is good, his love endures forever
8 136
Romans 8:31-35 - If God is for us, who can be against us ... who shall separate us from the love of God Christ?

Study Isaiah 48:8–11.

> [8] You have never heard, you have never known, from of old your ear has not been opened. For I knew that you would surely deal treacherously, and that from before birth you were called a rebel. [9] <u>For my name's sake</u> I defer my anger, for the sake of my praise I restrain it for you, that I may not cut you off. [10] Behold, I have refined you, but not as silver; I have tried you in the furnace of affliction. [11] <u>For my own sake, for my own sake,</u> I do it, for how should my name be profaned? My glory I will not give to another.

(also Romans 11:33-36)

Question 4: According to these verses, what is God passionate about? Underline phrases in this passage that support your answer.

Arguably, he <u>can't</u> compromise his glory,
he <u>won't</u> allow his glory to be tarnished
by our sin. So his passion for us sent
his son to die.

When we see that everything is done for his glory, it puts him in the center of everything, not us.

LESSON
2

DAY
3

> My conclusion is that God's own glory is uppermost in His own affections. In everything He does, His purpose is to preserve and display that glory. To say that His own glory is uppermost in His own affections means that He puts a greater value on it than on anything else. He delights in His glory above all things.[5]

DAY 3—PURSUING JOY

Blaise Pascal was a French mathematician who died in 1662. One of his most famous works was entitled "Pensees." The following paragraph from that work has had a profound influence on John Piper.

> All men seek happiness. This is without exception. Whatever different means they employ, they all tend to this end. The cause of some going to war, and of others avoiding it, is the same desire in both, attended with different views. This is the motive of every action of every man, even of those who hang themselves.[6]

Question 5: Interact with the above paragraph. Is it true that "all men seek happiness…without exception"? How is someone who hangs himself seeking happiness?

Probably, all sane people seek happiness. Some suffer for what they think is temporary to achieve happiness later. Insanity probably plays a part in some hanging, the loss of all hope for happiness others; maybe some think happiness will only come after death.

Go back to difference between happiness & joy.

Question 6: How do you think the Bible views the pursuit of happiness? Does the Bible endorse or condemn the pursuit of happiness? Cite Scripture in your answer.

Ecc. 5: 19 - ... L accept his lot & be happy in his work, this is a gift of God.

Psalm 37:4- delight yourself in the Lord & he will give you the desires of your heart.   *~verse supporting Westminster catechism~*

Psalm 119:24- Your statutes are my delight.   *~to enjoy God forever.~*

We are to pursue happiness in Christ & his laws

DAY 4—FALLING SHORT

Study Romans 1:18–25.

18 For the wrath of God is revealed from heaven against all ungodliness and unrighteousness of men, who by their unrighteousness suppress the truth. 19 For what can be known about God is plain to them, because God has shown it to them. 20 For his invisible attributes, namely, his eternal power and divine nature, have been clearly perceived, ever since the creation of the world, in the things that have been made. So they are without excuse. 21 For although they knew God, they did not honor him as God or give thanks to him, but they became futile in their thinking, and their foolish hearts were darkened. 22 Claiming to be wise, they became fools, 23 and exchanged the glory of the immortal God for images resembling mortal man and birds and animals and reptiles. 24 Therefore God gave them up in the lusts of their hearts to impurity, to the dishonoring of their bodies among themselves, 25 because they exchanged the truth about God for a lie and worshiped and served the creature rather than the Creator, who is blessed forever! Amen.

LESSON
2

DAY
4

Question 7: Underline all the words and phrases in the passage above that have to do with sin. From these words and phrases, come up with a brief working definition of sin.

Not honoring God as God, exchanging the glory of God for something else.

Examine Jeremiah 2:12–13.

> [12] Be appalled, O heavens, at this; be shocked, be utterly desolate, declares the LORD, [13] for my people have committed two evils: they have forsaken me, the fountain of living waters, and hewed out cisterns for themselves, broken cisterns that can hold no water.

Question 8*: To what is God compared in this passage? What two evils had God's people committed? If this is a description of evil, how should we understand what "good" is?

God is compared to living waters.
2 evils: 1) Forsaken God
          2) "Hewed" out broken cisterns that can hold no water.
Good could be defined as not forsaking God and turning to worthless idols; but trust in the fountain of living waters.

DAY 5—TO SERVE OR NOT TO SERVE?

Question 9: Is it biblical to attempt to serve God? Cite Scripture to show that God desires us to serve him.

Det. 10:12 - fear the Lord your God, to walk in all his ways, to
love him, to serve the Lord your God with all your
heart and with all your soul, and to observe the Lord's
commands.

Heb. 9:14 How much more then will the blood of Christ ... clean our
consciences from acts that lead to death so that we may

Consider Luke 4:8.   serve the living God.

Hebrews 12:1

8 And Jesus answered him, "It is written, 'You shall worship the Lord your God, and him only shall you serve.'"

Now consider Romans 12:11.

11 Do not be slothful in zeal, be fervent in spirit, serve the Lord.

Look at Mark 10:45.

45 "For even the Son of Man came not to be served but to serve, and to give his life as a ransom for many."

Look at Acts 17:24–25.

LESSON
2

DAY
5

24 The God who made the world and everything in it, being Lord of heaven and earth, does not live in temples made by man, 25 nor is he served by human hands, as though he needed anything, since he himself gives to all mankind life and breath and everything.

If we serve God as if he needed us. If we let him serve us,
he is magnified. 1 Peter 4:11 - we serve with the strength that God
provides so that he will get the glory. It's a miracle when we serve &
he gets the glory.

Question 10*: In the first set of verses, we are commanded to serve God. In the second set, we are told that "God is not served by human hands." How do we reconcile these two sets of verses? Should we or should we not serve God? Attempt to resolve this tension.

In Acts, the use of the word served means benefitted; God does not benefit or is helped in some way by our service, we receive the benefits. In Det. 10:13 (which I used above) it goes on to say ... "for your own good."
It pleases God when we serve him (Rom. 14:18).

FURTHER UP AND FURTHER IN

Note: The "Further Up and Further In" section is for those who want to study more. It is a section for further reference and going deeper. The phrase "further up and further in" is borrowed from C. S. Lewis.

Read John Piper's sermon "Is God For Us or For Himself?" at www.desiringgod.org/library/topics/gods_passion/god_us_himself.html.

Question 11: List all the texts in this sermon which demonstrate that God does all things for the sake of his glory.

God being for himself and for us go hand in hand. Why is it so important for his children to praise his glory? What is the best gift he can give us. Himself! By exalting himself and encouraging us to know him, we are given the best gift possible. Psalm 16:11 - in God's presence there is a fullness of joy. What do we do when we are given a great gift? We praise it & enjoy it. And in facts, praising something completes the joy. So if God is truly for us, if he would give us the best and make us joy full, he must make it his aim to get us to praise him. No because he needs it, but because it benefits us.

Read the Following Quote from Jonathan Edwards:

> So God glorifies Himself toward the creatures also in two ways: 1. By appearing to... their understanding. 2. In communicating Himself to their hearts, and in their rejoicing and delighting in, and enjoying, the manifestations which He makes of Himself.... God is glorified not only by His glory's being seen, but by its being rejoiced in. When those that see it delight in it, God is more glorified than if they only see it. His glory is then received by the whole soul, both by the understanding and by the heart. God made the world that He might communicate, and the creature receive, His glory; and that it might [be] received both by the mind and heart. He that testifies his idea of God's glory [doesn't] glorify God so much as he that testifies also his approbation of it and his delight in it.[7]

Question 12. According to Jonathan Edwards, what is the relationship between the glory of God and the happiness of human beings? Restate Edwards's conclusion in your own words.

God made the universe so that he might communicate his glory to us — he is more glorified when we see it _and_ delight in it than if we just recognize it.

Read the following quote from C.S. Lewis:

But the most obvious fact about praise—whether of God
or anything—strangely escaped me. I thought of it in
terms of compliment, approval, or the giving of honor. I
had never noticed that all enjoyment spontaneously
overflows into praise unless (sometimes even if) shyness or
the fear of boring others is deliberately brought in to check
it. The world rings with praise—lovers praising their
mistresses, readers their favorite poet, walkers praising the
countryside, players praising their favorite game—praise of
weather, wines, dishes, actors, horses, colleges, countries,
historical personages, children, flowers, mountains, rare
stamps, rare beetles, even sometimes politicians and
scholars...My whole, more general difficulty about the praise
of God depended on my absurdly denying to us, as regards
the supremely Valuable, what we delight to do, what indeed
we can't help doing, about everything else we value.

I think we delight to praise what we enjoy because the
praise not merely expresses, but completes the enjoyment; it
is its appointed consummation. It is not out of compliment
that lovers keep on telling one another how beautiful they
are, the delight is incomplete till it is expressed.[8]

Question 13: What was the "obvious fact about praise" that C.S. Lewis missed? Do you agree with his assessment of why we praise things? Provide examples that support your answer.

Praise not just expresses, but completes enjoyment. It is much more fun to share an experience with someone than to experience it alone. (i.e. rides at an amusement park, sunsets, etc.)

Read an article that summarizes what Christian hedonism is at http://www.desiringgod.org/library/what_we_believe/christian_hedonism.html.

Question 14: Reflect on the statement, "God is most glorified in you when you are most satisfied in him." Is this a true and biblical statement? Why or why not? What are the implications of this truth for your life? Record your reflections below.

We all make a god out of what we take the most pleasure in. When that god is God, we are glorifying him the most. Psalm 37:4 - "if they delight themselves in the Lord he will give them the desire of their heart" - When we delight ourselves in the Lord, our desires, what makes us happy, will be doing his will. We shouldn't tell people not to pursue happiness, we need to point them in the right direction of what will make them happy.

Read Philippians 1:19–23.

LESSON
2

*Further up
and
further in*

[19] …for I know that through your prayers and the help of the Spirit of Jesus Christ this will turn out for my deliverance, [20] as it is my eager expectation and hope that I will not be at all ashamed, but that with full courage now as always Christ will be honored in my body, whether by life

or by death. [21] For to me to live is Christ, and to die is gain. [22] If I am to live in the flesh, that means fruitful labor for me. Yet which I shall choose I cannot tell. [23] I am hard pressed between the two. My desire is to depart and be with Christ, for that is far better.

Question 15: According to this verse, how do you honor Christ by life? How do you honor Christ by death? (Hint: notice the word "for" in v. 21.) Does this verse support Christian Hedonism? If so, how?

In life, fruitful labor.

In death, Paul will be with Christ - that is his gain, what he looks for now too. His relationship with Christ is his most precious possession.

While You Watch the DVD, Take Notes

John Piper's mission statement:

To spread a _passion_ for the _supremacy_ of God in all things for the _joy_ of all peoples through Jesus Christ.

What is John Piper's answer to the question, "Should we serve God?"

We should serve him by the strength he provides for his glory.

What text has John Piper quoted most often before he preaches?

1 Peter 4:11

According to John Piper, "The _giver_ gets the glory."

So never serve as giving to God

What is John Piper's goal in life?

After You Watch the DVD, Discuss What You've Learned

1. Is there a conflict between a passion for the glory of God and a passion for our own joy? As Christians, is it right to say that we should make it our life's goal to be happy?

2. In light of the discussion on the DVD, should we seek to serve God? If so, how do we do this in such a way that we don't belittle him?

3. Do you agree that "the giver gets the glory?" Should we ever try to give anything to God?

After You Discuss, Make Application

1. What was the most meaningful part of this lesson for you? Was there a sentence, concept, or idea that really struck you? Why? Record your thoughts in the space below.

2. Devote at least ten minutes this week to meditating on the reality that God desires to glorify himself by fully satisfying you. Compose a prayer that reflects this truth and pray it to God.

LESSON
2

DVD
and
discussion

A PASSION FOR PRACTICAL HOLINESS

A Companion Study to *Battling Unbelief*, Session 2

LESSON OBJECTIVES

It is our prayer that after you have finished this lesson...

- You will have a better grasp of the doctrine of justification by faith alone.

- You will understand the importance and necessity of personal holiness.

- You will begin to grasp the relationship between faith and good works.

Before You Watch the DVD, Study and Prepare

DAY 1—WHAT IS HOLINESS?

Question 1*: How would you define or describe holiness? How should we understand the relationship between the holiness of God and our own practical holiness? Record your reflections.

1- Set apart, separate; 2- perfect in righteousness and purity

We are set apart to grow closer to God; one day our righteousness will be complete. Ex. A pencil is holy when it is used to serve God. We become holy by conforming to the image of Christ, through obedience.

Question 2: How crucial is it for Christians to be holy? What is at stake in the fight to become holy?

Heb. 12:14- without holiness we will not see the Lord. But this is done at the resurrection. 2 Peter 3 - we are not to put our future inheritance in this world that will be lost. Heb 12: 9-17 -if we belong to God he will chastise us when we stray, for our good.

DAY 2—JUSTIFIED BY FAITH ALONE

The full meaning of justification, as pardon and imputed perfection, has proved to be a mighty antidote to despair for the saints. John Bunyan, the author of *Pilgrim's Progress*, was tormented with uncertainty about his standing with God until this doctrine broke in on his soul. We know that our measure of obedience, even on our best days, falls short of this standard. Our hope for acceptance with God and eternal life is the provision of Christ.

Alongside the pastoral preciousness of the doctrine of the imputed righteousness of Christ is the great truth that this doctrine bestows on Jesus Christ the full honor that he deserves. Not only should he be honored as the one who died to pardon us, and not only should he be honored as the one who sovereignly works faith and obedience in us, but he should also be honored as the one who provided a perfect righteousness.[9]

LESSON

3

DAY

2

Read Romans 3:28.

28 For we hold that one is justified by faith apart from works of the law.

Look at Romans 5:1.

1 Therefore, since we have been justified by faith, we have peace with God through our Lord Jesus Christ.

Now look at Galatians 2:16.

16 ...yet we know that a person is not justified by works of the law but through faith in Jesus Christ, so we also have believed in Christ Jesus, in order to be justified by faith in Christ and not by works of the law, because by works of the law no one will be justified.

Question 3: What is the central point that is taught in these three verses? Why is this truth so important?

Justification by faith in Jesus Christ. We don't have to earn our salvation; we can be assured because we depend on the perfect works of Christ.

Read the following statement on "The Justifying Act of God" from section 9.1 of *The Bethlehem Baptist Church Elder Affirmation of Faith*:

> 9.1 We believe that in a free act of righteous grace God justifies the ungodly by faith alone apart from works, pardoning their sins, and reckoning them as righteous and acceptable in His presence. Faith is thus the sole instrument by which we, as sinners, are united to Christ, whose perfect righteousness and satisfaction for sins is alone the ground of our acceptance with God. This acceptance happens fully and permanently at the first instant of justification. Thus the righteousness by which we come into right standing with God is not anything worked in us by God, neither imparted to us at baptism nor over time, but rather is accomplished for us, outside ourselves, and is imputed to us.[10]

Question 4*: According to this summary statement of the doctrine of justification, when does justification occur? What is the ground of our justification? What is the means of our justification? Why is it important that our justification is not something that is worked in us?

Justification occurs at the time of faith and unity with Christ.

Our grounds of justification is the perfect righteousness and satisfaction of sins by Christ alone. The means of grace is though Christ imparting his righteousness to us. [If God worked it in us, it would change the gospel, and make us.]

DAY 3—THE NECESSITY OF HOLINESS

Read Hebrews 12:14.

[14] Strive for peace with everyone, and for the holiness without which no one will see the Lord.

LESSON
3

DAY
3

Now read John 5:28–29.

> [28] Do not marvel at this, for an hour is coming when all who are in the tombs will hear his voice [29] and come out, those who have done good to the resurrection of life, and those who have done evil to the resurrection of judgment.

Only those who are saved can truly do good.

Next, look at Matthew 6:14–15.

> [14] For if you forgive others their trespasses, your heavenly Father will also forgive you, [15] but if you do not forgive others their trespasses, neither will your Father forgive your trespasses.

Question 5: According to these passages, what is necessary if we are to "see the Lord," "come out...to a resurrection of life," and be forgiven for our trespasses?

Holiness, doing good, forgiving others

Examine Romans 8:13.

> [13] For if you live according to the flesh you will die, but if by the Spirit you put to death the deeds of the body, you will live.

Now examine Galatians 6:7–9.

> [7] Do not be deceived: God is not mocked, for whatever one sows, that will he also reap. [8] For the one who sows to his own flesh will from the flesh reap corruption, but the one who sows to the Spirit will from the Spirit reap eternal life. [9] And let us not grow weary of doing good, for in due season we will reap, if we do not give up. *sowing to the Spirit*

Question 6*: What are the connections between these two passages? What is at stake in these passages? Is it eternal life and eternal death? Explain your answer. What is meant by the word "corruption" in Galatians 6:8? (Hint: notice what "corruption" is contrasted with.)

We are to live by the Spirit - our eternity is at stake. Corruption is translated destruction in NIV.

DAY 4—WRESTLING WITH A BIBLICAL TENSION

The great error that I am trying to explode is the error that says, "Faith in God is one thing and the fight for holiness is another thing. You get your justification by faith, and you get your sanctification by works. You start the Christian life in the power of the Spirit, you press on in the efforts of the flesh. The battle for obedience is optional because only faith is necessary for final salvation." Faith alone is necessary for justification, but the purity that confirms faith's reality is also necessary for *final* salvation.[11]

LESSON
3

DAY
4

Question 7*: Do you detect a tension between the truth that we are justified by faith alone and the truth that practical holiness is necessary for final salvation? Describe this tension.

Question 8: Make an effort to resolve the tension that you described in Question 7.

Faith alone is necessary for salvation, but practical
holiness (works) is evidence that the faith is real.
Maybe who saying I'm a good ball player. If that is true,
my statistics will be good. The statistics don't define me as
a ball player, but they are evidence of it.

DAY 5—FAITH AND WORKS

Faith itself is the agent of the works. They do not merely accompany faith. They come through or by faith. Faith is the agent that produces the works. And it does so necessarily. Thus the works are evidence of true faith, and are not the means of our salvation the way faith is. They are the evidence that faith is real and thus are necessary for final salvation, though not the ground of it, as the death and righteousness of Christ are, or the means of it, as faith is.[12]

Question 9*: How should we understand the relationship between faith and works? Cite Scripture in your answer.

James 2: 14-26   Faith without works is dead. For Abraham (and sacrificing Isaac on the altar), "his faith and his actions were working together, and his faith was made complete by what he did."
Justification is just one link in the chain of God's redemption plan: It calls → he justifies → he glorifies (Romans 8:30)

Question 10: How is it that true faith produces good works? What is the dynamic that ensures that genuine, saving faith always brings forth works of faith?

Faith is the agent of good works. They do not merely accompany faith, they come through or by faith. And it does so necessarily. Works are necessary for final salvation, but they are not the ground of it (Christ) or the means of it — faith.

FURTHER UP AND FURTHER IN

The *Westminster Confession of Faith* is a classic summary of essential Christian truths. Study the following statement on justification from the *Westminster Confession of Faith*.

(1) Those whom God effectually calleth He also freely justifieth; not by infusing righteousness into them, but by pardoning their sins, and by accounting and accepting their persons as righteous: not for anything wrought in them, or done by them, but for Christ's sake alone...(2) Faith, thus receiving and resting on Christ and His righteousness, is the alone instrument of justification; yet is it not alone in the person justified, but is ever accompanied with all other saving graces, and is no dead faith, but worketh by love.[13]

LESSON
3

Further up and further in

LESSON
3

Further up
and
further in

Question 11: Summarize this section from the *Westminster Confession* in your own words.

(1) Those called by God are justified by forgiving our sins, not because of what was accomplished in us or by us, but for Jesus Christ's sake alone. (2) Faith is the only means of justification, and it does not exist alone but is accompanied by the reaction of a person saved.

Read Romans 8:28–30.

28 And we know that for those who love God all things work together for good, for those who are called according to his purpose. 29 For those whom he foreknew he also predestined to be conformed to the image of his Son, in order that he might be the firstborn among many brothers. 30 And those whom he predestined he also called, and those whom he called he also justified, and those whom he justified he also glorified.

Now read John 10:27–30.

27 My sheep hear my voice, and I know them, and they follow me. 28 I give them eternal life, and they will never perish, and no one will snatch them out of my hand. 29 My Father, who has given them to me, is greater than all, and no one is able to snatch them out of the Father's hand. 30 I and the Father are one.

Question 12: According to these texts, is it possible for a genuine believer in Jesus Christ to fail to attain eternal life? Can a Christian lose their salvation? Can Christ lose a Christian?

Nope. Nope. Nope.

Investigate Galatians 5:19–21.

[19] Now the works of the flesh are evident: sexual immorality, impurity, sensuality, [20] idolatry, sorcery, enmity, strife, jealousy, fits of anger, rivalries, dissensions, divisions, [21] envy, drunkenness, orgies, and things like these. I warn you, as I warned you before, that those who do such things will not inherit the kingdom of God.

Now read Hebrews 6:4–6.

[4] For it is impossible to restore again to repentance those who have once been enlightened, who have tasted the heavenly gift, and have shared in the Holy Spirit, [5] and have tasted the goodness of the word of God and the powers of the age to come, [6] if they then fall away, since they are crucifying once again the Son of God to their own harm and holding him up to contempt.

Next, Matthew 7:21–23.

[21] "Not everyone who says to me, 'Lord, Lord,' will enter the kingdom of heaven, but the one who does the will of my Father who is in heaven. [22] On that day many will say to me, 'Lord, Lord, did we not prophesy in your name, and cast out demons in your name, and do many mighty works in your name?' [23] And then will I declare to them, 'I never knew you; depart from me, you workers of lawlessness.'"

LESSON
3

Further up and further in

Question 13: In light of the fact that all those who are justified are glorified (Romans 8:30), how should we understand the three passages above that warn Christians of the terrible consequences of falling away from faith?

Faith that leads to no good works is essentially dead - not true faith. These passages are meant to highlight this fact, not replace salvation through faith with salvation through works

Read Section 10 of *The Bethlehem Baptist Church Elder Affirmation of Faith* entitled "God's Work in Faith and Sanctification" at www.bbcmpls.org/aboutus/documents/AOFwithESV4-20-04.pdf.

Question 14: In your own words, summarize the four reasons that justifying faith necessarily sanctifies.

1) Justifying faith is a persevering faith.
2) Justifying faith trusts in the fulfillment of all God's promises
3) Justifying faith embraces Christ in all his roles (including Guide, teacher, helper, etc. - not just part of him.
4) Embracing all of Christ is heartfelt & Spirit given,

Question 15: According to the *Elder Affirmation of Faith*, is it possible for a genuine believer in Jesus to fall away from the faith and perish eternally? What ensures that Christians will persevere to the end?

all of this results in a transformed life.

Justifying faith results in an immediate, and permanent acceptance by God. It is not something worked in us but is accomplished outside of us and imputed to us. Justification is not God making us holy, it is a legal declaration where from that time God regards us as if we were perfectly righteous

While You Watch the DVD, Take Notes

[handwritten: 2 Thes 2:13 – God has chosen us to Salvation through sanctification.]

How does John Piper describe holiness?

1. *[handwritten: Obedience to God's word]*
2. *[handwritten: Fruit of the Holy Spirit]*
3. *[handwritten: Genuine love for other people]* *[handwritten: (1 Thes 3:12-13)]*

What problem is raised by the necessity of holiness for final salvation?

We are *[handwritten: justified]* by faith alone, but that faith never

_____ _____.

[handwritten: Why does justifying faith a]

What analogy does John Piper give to describe the relationship
between faith and good works?

[handwritten: Baby – who was the mother. Solomon said divide the baby the true mother said don't kill it. Solomon was not worthy]

How does faith accomplish the work of sanctification? *[handwritten: for a dead that.]*

[handwritten: It saves the rest of sin by embracing a better future and offering a superior satisfaction.]

[handwritten: would earn the child,]

After You Watch the DVD, Discuss What You've Learned *[handwritten: he was worthy for a dead]*

1. What is the relationship between holiness and love? How does *[handwritten: that]*
    this understanding of holiness compare to any previous *[handwritten: is already]*
    ideas you have had about holiness? *[handwritten: true.]*

2 . Discuss the tension between justification by faith alone
    and the necessity of good works for final salvation. Do
    you think the solution proposed by John Piper and the
    Westminster Confession of Faith resolves this tension? If
    possible, use Scripture to defend your answer.

LESSON

3

*DVD
and
discussion*

3. How does the analogy of Solomon and the two women help us understand the relationship between faith and good works? Is the analogy a good one? Can you think of another analogy that would illustrate the same point?

After You Discuss, Make Application

1. What was the most meaningful part of this lesson for you? Was there a sentence, concept, or idea that really struck you? Why? Record your thoughts in the space below.

2. At some point this week, discuss with a friend that personal holiness is necessary for final salvation. Then discuss how this truth relates to the doctrine of justification by faith alone. Record important parts of the conversation below.

If we are justified by grace through faith

IS IT BIBLICAL?
(PART 1)

A Companion Study to *Battling Unbelief*, Session 3

LESSON OBJECTIVES

It is our prayer that after you have finished this lesson...

- You will understand how sanctification differs from justification.

- You will begin to see grace not just as pardon from sin, but as power over sin also.

- You will see the importance of the future orientation of faith.

Before You Watch the DVD, Study and Prepare

DAY 1—SANCTIFICATION AND GRACE

Progressive holiness

Question 1*: Define sanctification. Think of some synonyms for sanctification. How does sanctification differ from justification?

The process of conforming to the image of Christ by the work of the Spirit in us. Justification is a legal ruling of God at one point in time where he declares us righteous, sanctification is an ongoing process within us to make us holy

Question 2: A proper understanding of the grace of God is absolutely essential for the Christian life. Give your own definition of grace. Use Scripture in your answer.

Unmerited gifts from God. Deut 7:6-8 - Israel was chosen because God loved them. Romans 3:19-24 - Righteousness is a gift from God, we cannot boast. Romans 4:4-8 - When a man works his wages are not a gift, but our justification is not done by works

DAY 2—WHAT GRACE DOES

Study 2 Corinthians 8:1–3.

Grace - bestowing something you don't deserve
Mercy - withholding something you do deserve

[1] We want you to know, brothers, about the grace of God that has been given among the churches of Macedonia, [2] for in a severe test of affliction, their abundance of joy and their extreme poverty have overflowed in a wealth of generosity on their part. [3] For they gave according to their means, as I can testify, and beyond their means, of their own free will,

Question 3*: According to this passage, what does grace produce when it lands on a church? In your mind, what is the most striking thing about this passage?

Abundance of joy & generosity. That these were evident during a severe test of affliction.
It doesn't remove affliction, but it produces joy.
It doesn't take away poverty, but it produces wealth of generosity

All of Paul's letters begin and end in a similar fashion. The following passages from 1 Corinthians are exemplary of the way that Paul begins and ends each of his letters.

1 Corinthians 1:3:

> 3 Grace to you and peace from God our Father and the Lord Jesus Christ.

1 Corinthians 16:23:

> 23 The grace of the Lord Jesus be with you.

Question 4: What is the significance of the fact that Paul begins and ends each of his letters in this way? What is he trying to communicate to his readers?

That all he is about to say and all he has said is predicated on the grace of God.

DAY 3—UNDERSTANDING GRACE AND FAITH

Read 2 Corinthians 12:7–9.

> 7 So to keep me from being too elated by the surpassing greatness of the revelations, a thorn was given me in the flesh, a messenger of Satan to harass me, to keep me from being too elated. 8 Three times I pleaded with the Lord about this, that it should leave me. 9 But he said to me, "My grace is sufficient for you, for my power is made perfect in weakness." Therefore I will boast all the more gladly of my weaknesses, so that the power of Christ may rest upon me.

LESSON
4

DAY
3

Question 5: How is grace described in this passage? Underline key phrases. What was Paul's reaction to God's response in v. 9? How does this understanding of grace compare to your definition in Question 2?

The all-sufficient power of Christ within us.
He was content more gladly of his weaknesses.

Question 6*: Provide your own working definition of faith. Cite Scripture in your answer. According to your definition, is faith mainly past, present, or future-oriented?

Faith is being sure of what we hope for and certain of what we do not see. (Heb 11:1)

Faith is maintaining a belief in something that cannot be proved.

DAY 4—SEEING THE DIVINE DESIGN
IN SUFFERING

Study 2 Corinthians 1:8–9.

8 For we do not want you to be ignorant, brothers, of the affliction we experienced in Asia. For we were so utterly burdened beyond our strength that we despaired of life itself. 9 Indeed, we felt that we had received the sentence of death. But that was to make us rely not on ourselves but on God who raises the dead.

Question 7*: According to this passage, what was the divine design behind Paul's suffering? What is the significance of this truth for your life?

To make them rely not on theirselves but on God.
It should move me to rest in the sovereignty of God and the
all sufficient power of Christ in me (grace) even when things aren't
going well.

Question 8: How does suffering work to produce faith? Cite Scripture in your answer.

James 1:2-3 (see below) We look for hope during suffering, most
people can survive affliction as long as there's hope that it
will end. Our hope is in eternal life, and it is during affliction we focus
on that hope.
1 Peter 1:6-8

Strange as it may seem, one of the primary purposes of being shaken by suffering is to make our faith more unshakable. Faith in future grace is like muscle tissue: if you stress it to the limit, it gets stronger, not weaker. That's what James means when he says, "Consider it all joy, my brethren, when you encounter various trials, knowing that the testing of your faith produces endurance" (James 1:2–3). When your faith is threatened and tested and stretched to the breaking point, the result is greater capacity to endure.[14]

LESSON

4

DAY

4

DAY 5—GRACE AND GLORY

LESSON 4

DAY 5

Examine 2 Corinthians 4:13–18.

13 Since we have the same spirit of <u>faith</u> according to what has been written, "I believed, and so I spoke," we also believe, and so we also speak, 14 knowing that he who raised the Lord Jesus will raise us also with Jesus and bring us with you into his presence. 15 For it is all for your sake, so that as <u>grace</u> extends to more and more people it may increase thanksgiving, to the <u>glory</u> of God. 16 So we do not lose heart. Though our outer nature is wasting away, our inner nature is being renewed day by day. 17 For this slight momentary affliction is preparing for us an eternal weight of <u>glory</u> beyond all comparison, 18 as we look not to the things that are seen but to the things that are unseen. For the things that are seen are transient, but the things that are unseen are eternal.

Question 9*: Underline every occurrence of the words "grace," "faith," and "glory" in this passage. Summarize this passage in your own words. Be sure to mention whether faith is past or future-oriented.

When we believe, we tell others. As we die to ourselves, we are inwardly renewed to God. And any affliction faced now points to our eternal rewards in heaven.

Question 10: According to this passage, how does grace glorify God? What is faith in future grace producing in the life of Paul?

Because as people recognize the grace of God, they give him thanks and tell other people.

FURTHER UP AND FURTHER IN

Ponder Philippians 2:12–13.

> [12] Therefore, my beloved, as you have always obeyed, so now, not only as in my presence but much more in my absence, work out your own salvation with fear and trembling, [13] for it is God who works in you, both to will and to work for his good pleasure.

Question 11: Does the fact that God "works in us to will and to work for his good pleasure" absolve us of the responsibility to act and demonstrate our salvation? If God is going to work in us, what is our responsibility?

No, it is our responsibility to obey God as he works in us to change us into who we should be.

Question 12: According to this passage, what is the relationship between our work and God's work in us? Which is more foundational? Why is this truth so crucial for our lives?

God works in us to change our will to match his, and to work for his good pleasure. We can't change our will (and act) without his working in us.

Study Hebrews 11 in your own Bible.

LESSON
4

Further up and further in

Question 13: What kinds of things did faith produce in the saints spoken of in Hebrews 11? Was their faith past-oriented or future-oriented? Why do you think this is significant? Record your reflections on this chapter in the space below.

Noah - warned about things not seen built on ark
Abraham - went when called even though he didn't know where he was
        going.
vs 13 - they did not recieve the things promised, they welcomed them from
        a distance.
vs 39 - none received what was promised

Read the following statement on "God's Work in Faith and Sanctification" from section 10.1 of *The Bethlehem Baptist Church Elder Affirmation of Faith*:

> We believe that justification and sanctification are both brought about by God through faith, but not in the same way. Justification is an act of God's imputing and reckoning; sanctification is an act of God's imparting and transforming. Thus the function of faith in regard to each is different. In regard to justification, faith is not the channel through which power or transformation flows to the soul of the believer, but rather faith is the occasion of God's forgiving, acquitting, and reckoning as righteous. But in regard to sanctification, faith is indeed the channel through which divine power and transformation flow to the soul; and the sanctifying work of God through faith does indeed touch the soul and change it into the likeness of Christ.[15]

Question 14: In your own words, what is the crucial difference between how faith functions in justification and sanctification? Why is this distinction so important? What happens if we lose this distinction?

In justification, faith, which comes from God, is not a conduit for something to flow from God to us, it is just the event that describes God's looking at us in a new way. For sanctification, it is the conduit through which he infuses us with holiness.

Question 15: Is it right to say that God ordains suffering in the world? How would you respond to someone who said, "God doesn't ordain suffering; he simply does the best he can with what he's given"? Cite Scripture in your answer.

God does ordain suffering; to say he doesn't diminishes his sovereignty.

Amos 3:6 disaster to a city, has not the Lord caused it

Isaiah 45:7 - I bring prosperity and create disaster.

Psalm 71:20 - You have made me see troubles, many & bitter.

While You Watch the DVD, Take Notes

Faith is the ___great___ ___worker___.

What is John Piper's definition of grace? *Disposition to save the unworthy and the power to bless us with the future with all that we need*

Ever-working power of God to meet our spiritual needs.

According to John Piper, why does Paul begin and end his letters in the way that he does? *Grace to you (beginning)* *"all" Grace with you (end)*

Grace to you though the letter while it is being read, and grace to go with them as he leaves."

What biblical texts demonstrate that faith is not merely about the past accomplishments of Christ, but also embraces a future governed by God's grace?

Heb. 11:1, Rom 4:16-24, Col 1:22-23, John 14:1, 2 Cor. 1:8-9

According to John Piper, how should we pray if we want to know the sweetness of fellowship with Christ?

Get pictures of how he ought to be and what the sweetness of fellowship ought to be - whatever it takes to be free from lust, greed, etc., to be a loving, good child of God, do it for me.

LESSON
4

*DVD
and
discussion*

After You Watch the DVD, Discuss What You've Learned

1. How was John Piper's definition of grace similar to your own? How was it different? How was it similar to other definitions of grace that you have heard?

2. Why is it so crucial that we grasp the future orientation of faith? Do you think that emphasizing this future orientation of faith minimizes the centrality of the past work of Jesus on the cross? Why or why not?

3. Is there a divine design in our suffering? How does faith in future grace enable us to endure every trial that we face?

After You Discuss, Make Application

1. What was the most meaningful part of this lesson for you? Was there a sentence, concept, or idea that really struck you? Why? Record your thoughts in the space below.

2. How does knowing that God has provided grace to meet all of your needs in the future affect your thinking about your:

   a. finances;
   b. marriage;
   c. job/school?

2 Cor. 9:8 - one of the greatest promises in the bible. How would our lives be different if we truly believed this? God will provide at this moment, tomorrow at the MRI, and 10 years when cancer takes over our body

IS IT BIBLICAL? (PART 2)

A Companion Study to *Battling Unbelief*, Session 4

LESSON OBJECTIVES

It is our prayer that after you have finished this lesson…

- You will understand the crucial function of past grace.

- You will grasp the danger of the debtor's ethic.

- You will understand the role of the Holy Spirit in enabling obedience.

Before You Watch the DVD, Study and Prepare

DAY 1—BYGONE GRACE

LESSON 5

DAY 1

Question 1*: If faith is fundamentally oriented toward future grace, what is the role of past grace in our lives?

Past grace - Christ's work on the cross, is fundamental to our justification. Past grace shown to us in our life strengthen our confidence of God's work in our lives.

> Confidence in someone's future reliability is grounded in a history of past faithfulness.[16]

Question 2: Do you agree with this statement? Can you think of an example of a time when someone's past faithfulness affects how we view their future reliability? Does this principle hold true with God as well? Cite Scripture in your answer.

> Bygone grace is the foundation for faith in future grace. We obey the teachings of Jesus by faith in future grace; and we lay hold on future grace in the promises of God's Word. But we certify the surety of the promises with the evidence of past grace. This past grace is God's down payment on the fullness of future grace.[17]

DAY 2—THE MOST PRECIOUS VERSE IN THE BIBLE

Study Romans 8:32.   *A*

> [32] He who did not spare his own Son but gave him up for us all, how will he not also with him graciously give us all things?

Question 3*: For John Piper, Romans 8:32 is "the most precious verse in the Bible."[18] What do you think makes this verse so precious? Explain the logic of the verse. Which is the more difficult thing for God to do: give us all things or not spare his own Son?

It shows both the past and present aspects of grace. It is a basis for every decision we make & how we live our lives; because if we truly believe God will give us all things necessary, then sinful ways that spring out of self-serving goals are not necessary

Question 4: What is included in the "all things" that God will give us? How can we be sure that God will indeed give us all things?

All things necessary are for our good. Because he said he would and he is faithful and true.

A ficiadio "from the greater to the lesser"
If God gave up his son (the greater), he will certainly give us all things (the lesser)
Think of a train loaded with our sins climbing to the top of a mountain & the power of the cross vs the peak of the mountain. Once you've past that point, you just hop on that train & ride it down into heaven

LESSON
5

DAY
2

LESSON 5

DAY 3

Romans 8:32 contains a foundation and guarantee that is so strong and so solid and so secure that there is absolutely no possibility that the promise could ever be broken. . . This verse is the most precious verse in the Bible to me because the foundation of the all-encompassing promise of future grace is that the Son of God bore in his body all my punishment and all my guilt and all my condemnation and all my blame and all my fault and all my corruption, so that I might stand before a great and holy God, forgiven, reconciled, justified, accepted, and the beneficiary of unspeakable promises of pleasure forever and ever at his right hand.[19]

Don't say I thank you for what you are going to do — say I trust in what you will do.

DAY 3—GRATITUDE AND THE DEBTOR'S ETHIC

Question 5: Define gratitude. What is the role of gratitude in motivating obedience? Cite Scripture in your answer.

Gratitude - appreciation for something received

See ~~verse~~ question 15.

Nowhere in the Bible is gratitude associated with obedience.

Gratitude is always looking back at God's accumulated history of grace. Faith is listening to him says things what gratitude is saying, I will give the future.

Question 6*: Sometimes Christians say things like, "God has done so much for me. Now it is my duty to do so much for him." What, if anything, is wrong with this statement? Should Christians speak this way? Why or why not?

We don't do things for him, as if we are repaying a debt.

We do things because we rejoice in all he has done for us

There is an impulse in the fallen human heart—all our hearts—to forget that gratitude is a spontaneous response of joy to receiving something over and above what we paid for. When we forget this, what happens is that gratitude starts to be misused and distorted as an impulse to pay for the very thing that came to us "gratis." This terrible moment is the birthplace of the "debtor's ethic."

The debtor's ethic says, "Because you have done something good for me, I feel indebted to do something good for you." This impulse is *not* what gratitude was designed to produce. God meant gratitude to be a spontaneous expression of pleasure in the gift and good will of another. He did not mean it to be an impulse to return favors. If gratitude is twisted into a sense of debt, it gives birth to the debtor's ethic—and the effect is to nullify grace.[20]

DAY 4—DEFINING FAITH

Read James 2:19.

[19] You believe that God is one; you do well. Even the demons believe—and shudder!

Question 7: Is it possible to have saving faith without a heartfelt desire for God? Is faith merely a mental assent to historical truths? What is the essential difference between the "faith" of demons and the faith of Christians?

LESSON
5

DAY
4

Demons don't have faith, they believe. Faith in the historical sense is God's justifying us though Christ's work on the cross. In the present sense, it is God's blessing us as we grow to be more like him. In the future sense, it is our hope of eternal life with him.

Read John 6:35.

> 35 Jesus said to them, "I am the bread of life; whoever comes to me shall not hunger, and whoever believes in me shall never thirst."

Now read Hebrews 11:6.

> 6 And without faith it is impossible to please him, for whoever would draw near to God must believe that he exists and that he rewards those who seek him.

Question 8*: From these verses, compose a definition of faith. How do hunger and thirst relate to faith?

Faith is the belief that God exists, and that he rewards us if we seek him (see #7 too).

Faith is also being satisfied with all that God is to us, not just an assent to him.

DAY 5—THE ROLE OF THE SPIRIT

Study John 16:13–14.

> 13 When the Spirit of truth comes, he will guide you into all the truth, for he will not speak on his own authority, but whatever he hears he will speak, and he will declare to you the things that are to come. 14 He will glorify me, for he will take what is mine and declare it to you.

Question 9: What is the role of the Spirit in this verse? What is the aim of the Spirit in fulfilling this role?

Guidinges into all truth. Its aim is to glorify God by revealing God to us.

Read Galatians 5:5–6.

> 5 For through the Spirit, by faith, we ourselves eagerly wait for the hope of righteousness. 6 For in Christ Jesus neither circumcision nor uncircumcision counts for anything, but only faith working through love.

Now compare that teaching to Galatians 5:22–23.

> 22 But the fruit of the Spirit is love, joy, peace, patience, kindness, goodness, faithfulness, 23 gentleness, self-control; against such things there is no law.

Question 10*: According to these verses, which produces love, the Spirit or faith? Describe how these two work together.

Both. By faith, the Spirit ~~works~~ works.

Gal. 3:5 "Does he who provides you with the spirit, ... does he do it by works or by faith."

Faith is the channel that the Spirit works through.

LESSON
5

DAY
5

FURTHER UP AND FURTHER IN

LESSON

5

*Further up
and
further in*

There is a sense in which gratitude and faith are interwoven joys that strengthen each other. As gratitude joyfully revels in the benefits of past grace, so faith joyfully relies on the benefits of future grace. Therefore when gratitude for God's past grace is strong, the message is sent that God is supremely trustworthy in the future because of what he has done in the past. In this way faith is strengthened by a lively gratitude for God's past trustworthiness.

On the other hand, when faith in God's future grace is strong, the message is sent that this kind of God makes no mistakes, so that everything he has done in the past is part of a good plan and can be remembered with gratitude. In this way gratitude is strengthened by a lively faith in God's future grace. Surely it is only the heart of faith in future grace that can follow the apostle Paul in "giving thanks for *all things* in the name of our Lord Jesus Christ" (Ephesians 5:20). Only if we trust God to turn past calamities into future comfort can we look back with gratitude for *all things*.

It seems to me that this interwovenness of future-oriented faith and past-oriented gratitude is what prevents gratitude from degenerating into the debtor's ethic. Gratitude for bygone grace is constantly saying to faith, "Be strong, and do not doubt that God will be as gracious in the future as I know he's been in the past." And faith in future grace is constantly saying to gratitude, "There is more grace to come, and all our obedience is to be done in reliance on future grace. Relax and exult in your appointed feast. I will take responsibility for tomorrow's obedience."[21]

Question 11: According to John Piper, what is the relationship between gratitude and faith? How do they strengthen each other?

Gratitude for God's past grace, faith is strengthened by the message that God will be supremely trustworthy in the future. When faith in the future is strong, it helps us realize all things in the past are for our good.

Examine Romans 5:9–10.

the greatest

lives

the greatest

Since, therefore, we have now been <u>justified by his blood,</u> much more shall we be saved by him <u>from the wrath of God.</u> ¹⁰ For if while we were enemies we were reconciled to God by the death of his Son, much more, now that we are reconciled, shall we be saved by his life.

Now examine Hebrews 4:14–16.

¹⁴ Since then (we have a great high priest) who has passed <u>through</u> the heavens, Jesus, the Son of God, (let us hold fast our confession.) ¹⁵ For we do not have a high priest who is unable to sympathize with our weaknesses, but one who in every respect <u>has been tempted</u> as we are, yet without sin. ¹⁶ Let us then with confidence (draw near to the throne of grace) that we (may receive mercy and find grace) to help in time of need.

Question 12: Underline all the phrases in these passages that relate to the past. Circle all the phrases that relate to the present or future. According to these passages, how does the past work of Jesus motivate us to trust in future grace?

Because Christ has been tempted

Question 13: Imagine that someone gives you a new home as a gift, with the condition that you must ask them to do any maintenance on the house. Make a list of ways that you could respond to them such that you nullify the graciousness of their gift. How could you respond to them in such a way that their graciousness is magnified?

Nullify:

1) Complain about the house - not be happy about it

Magnify:
1) Rejoice in the gift and enjoy it.

Wrestle with Psalm 116:12–13.

> [12] What shall I render to the LORD for all his benefits to me?
> [13] I will lift up the cup of salvation and call on the name of the LORD.

Question 14: How does the psalmist plan to "pay God back" for everything he has done for him? Is this the same as the "debtor's ethic?" Why or why not?

He will rejoice in his salvation & call on the name of God. This is not the response of paying God back, but rejoicing in what he has done and resting on his future promises

Question 15: Using a concordance, look up all the instances of words related to gratitude in the Bible (for example, "thanks," "thanksgiving," "grateful," etc.). List any verses that make gratitude the motivation for obedience in the Christian life. Based on your search, do you agree with John Piper that "the Bible rarely, if ever, motivates Christian living with gratitude"?[22]

While You Watch the DVD, Take Notes

Explain the logic of Romans 8:32 according to John Piper.

Faith is ✗ being _satisfied_ with all that God is for us in Jesus.

Why does the Spirit unite himself to faith as the way of bringing about works of love? *Why change it. if god loved us and we become a better person, so that why faith Spirit is, love is produced. It is because as the fundamental mission of the spirit given in John 16 – he will glorify God.*

Give three reasons why it is dangerous to try and pay God back *The spirit produces love through faith in Jesus. Memorize Matt 6:25-34*

1. *We can never pay him back (1 Cor 15:10, it is not I) we must*
2. *remain a debtor to grace forever*
3. *Grace is free or it's not grace*

Paying back is basing on the bygone grace, not looking forward to future grace.

You can't run your car on gratitude for yesterday's grace.

After You Watch the DVD, Discuss What You've Learned

1. Discuss the relationship between bygone grace and future grace.

2. Do you agree with John Piper's definition of faith as "being satisfied with all that God is for us in Jesus"? Defend your answer.

LESSON 5

DVD and discussion

3. Discuss the relationship between gratitude and faith. Describe the dangers of the "payback" mentality. Have you ever fallen into this way of thinking? What was the result?

After You Discuss, Make Application

1. What was the most meaningful part of this lesson for you? Was there a sentence, concept, or idea that really struck you? Why? Record your thoughts in the space below.

2. This week, explain to a friend why it is wrong and dangerous to try to pay God back for his grace. Be sure to explain how faith in future grace is different from the payback mentality. Record your conversation below.

ORIGINS OF RADICAL LOVE (PART 1)

A Companion Study to *Battling Unbelief*, Session 5

LESSON OBJECTIVES

It is our prayer that after you have finished this lesson…

- You will begin to see how faith in future grace produces love.

- You will understand the difference between a legalistic and a faith-based approach to obedience.

- You will receive grace from God, enabling you to be a more loving person.

Before You Watch the DVD, Study and Prepare

DAY 1—EXAMINING OUR MOTIVATION

LESSON 6

DAY 1

Question 1: Think of a time in your life when you engaged in an act of sacrificial love for someone else. What led you to do this? What was the motivation behind your love?

Question 2*: What, if anything, is wrong with saying, "What motivates me to radical acts of sacrificial love is my desire to be as happy as I can?" Is it selfish to serve others for the joy that serving brings?

Because the focus is not on God, or even on others that we are serving, the focus is on us

DAY 2—FAITH AND REWARD-SEEKING

Study Hebrews 11:6.

> [6] And without faith it is impossible to please him, for whoever would draw near to God must believe that he exists and that he rewards those who seek him.

Now study Matthew 5:10–12.

[10] Blessed are those who are persecuted for righteousness' sake, for theirs is the kingdom of heaven. [11] Blessed are you when others revile you and persecute you and utter all kinds of evil against you falsely on my account. [12] Rejoice and be glad, for your reward is great in heaven, for so they persecuted the prophets who were before you.

Question 3*: According to these verses, how does reward-seeking relate to faith? In light of these passages, is it right to say "In order to please God, we must seek reward above all else"? Defend your answer.

It is impossible to receive rewards from God without faith. Those who are persecuted for their faith will receive a great reward. Hebrews says he rewards those who seek him. we do not seek rewards but God.

Question 4: If faith at its essence is coming to God for the reward he offers, does this make faith a mercenary affair? In other words, if we define faith as "coming to God for reward," are we just using God for our own self-interest? Explain your answer.

Faith is not coming to God for rewards, it is belief in God and his sovereign power.

LESSON
6

DAY
2

DAY 3—WHAT ABOUT SELF-DENIAL?

LESSON 6

DAY 3

Consider Luke 9:23–25.

23 And he said to all, "If anyone would come after me, let him deny himself and take up his cross daily and follow me. 24 For whoever would save his life will lose it, but whoever loses his life for my sake will save it. 25 For what does it profit a man if he gains the whole world and loses or forfeits himself?"

Question 5*: How do we reconcile reward-seeking faith with Jesus' call for self-denial in the passage above? How can we obey this command if saving faith includes seeking reward from God?

Question 6: As Christians, are we ever called to engage in *ultimate* self-denial? Why or why not?

DAY 4—LOVING OUR ENEMIES

Question 7*: Think about a time when someone has treated you poorly. What is your natural instinct in those situations? How do you regard the person who has treated you badly?

To get mad & verbally attack them. I guess at that particular moment they are my enemy.

Question 8: How does Jesus call us to respond to people who have treated us badly? How are we to treat those who persecute us? Cite Scripture in your answer.

Love them Luke 6:27 "Love your enemies, do good to those who hate you; bless those who curse you, pray for those who mistreat you."

Romans 12:20/Proverbs 25:21 - "If your enemy is hungry, feed him; If he is thirsty, give him something to drink."

DAY 5—ASK, SEEK, KNOCK

Read Matthew 7:7–12.

> [7] Ask, and it will be given to you; seek, and you will find; knock, and it will be opened to you. [8] For everyone who asks receives, and the one who seeks finds, and to the one who knocks it will be opened. [9] Or which one of you, if his son asks him for bread, will give him a stone? [10] Or if he asks for a fish, will give him a serpent? [11] If you then, who are evil, know how to give good gifts to your children, how much more will your Father who is in heaven give good things to those who ask him! [12] So whatever you wish that others would do to you, do also to them, for this is the Law and the Prophets.

LESSON 6

DAY 5

Question 9*: How should we understand unanswered prayer in light of this verse?

That ultimately the thing we prayed for was not for our good. When we trust in the Bible, we pray for what we need, God will always give you what you ask for (or something better). 3 yr. old asks for cracker, but it has mold on it. Father won't give him a moldy cracker, but will give him something better instead.

Question 10: What is the connection between 7:7–11 and 7:12? (Hint: notice the word "so.") Explain the logic of this passage.

FURTHER UP AND FURTHER IN

Question 11: Define the term "legalism." In your mind, what is the difference between a legalistic approach to obedience and a faith-based approach? Give an example of each.

Legalism = do something for something.
without commit. directly, I can do it, I will try
my hardest
Faith based - God, I know I can't do that, I pray for the
strength of your spirit in me to help.

Study Matthew 22:35–40.

35 And one of them, a lawyer, asked him a question to test him. 36 "Teacher, which is the great commandment in the Law?" 37 And he said to him, "You shall love the Lord your God with all your heart and with all your soul and with all your mind. 38 This is the great and first commandment. 39 And a second is like it: You shall love your neighbor as yourself. 40 On these two commandments depend all the Law and the Prophets."

Question 12: Does this passage (particularly v. 39) indicate that it is right for Christians to love themselves? In other words, is self-love wrong?

It implies that we do love ourselves, the command is to love others equally.

Question 13: In his book *Desiring God*, John Piper writes that "the pursuit of pleasure is an essential motive for every good deed."[23] Do you agree or disagree with this statement? Explain your answer.

Similar to question 5, pg 12.

Read the letter from Ronn in *Desiring God*, Chapter 4, Page 133[24]

Question 14: Do you agree or disagree with Ronn's analysis of the two situations he mentions? Explain your answer.

I disagree because both of the acts listed are short term. Christ knew what would result from his suffering, and that his father's love and will would ultimately prove the most joyous way.

LESSON
6

*Further up
and
further in*

Read John Piper's response to Ronn's letter in *Desiring God*,
chapter 4, pages 134–136

Question 15: Evaluate John Piper's response. Do you believe
that he adequately answered Ronn's objections? Would you
have responded differently? If so, how?

*this we need the Holy
Spirit for, to remind us
our reward is in
heaven*

this is error

While You Watch the DVD, Take Notes

we are wired to be negative toward those who are negative to us

According to John Piper, is it easier to <u>rejoice in your suffering</u> or to
<u>pray for your enemies</u>?

*Matt. 5:43 – love/pray for your enemies. How?   ? Matthew 5:10 – we can be happy
because our reward in heaven*

What is the difference between a legalistic and a faith-based
approach to obedience? *Legalist attacks command directly, faith says no
way, I can't do that*

What is John Piper's solution to the problem of unanswered prayer?

What word does John Piper focus on in Matthew 7:7–12?
therefore

Where does obedience to the Golden Rule come from? *points
to the fact that God will give "good things" to those who ask him*

After You Watch the DVD, Discuss What You've Learned

1. Give an example from your life when faith in future grace freed
   you to love someone. Describe your thinking in that moment.

2. How does the promise of future reward free us to rejoice in suf-fering and love in hard places?

3. Discuss John Piper's solution to the problem of unanswered prayer. Do you agree with his solution? Do you have another solution?

After You Discuss, Make Application

1. What was the most meaningful part of this lesson for you? Was there a sentence, concept, or idea that really struck you? Why? Record your thoughts in the space below.

2. Write down a very specific prayer request for yourself or for someone close to you. Over the next few weeks, watch to see how that prayer is answered in the way you expect or in a way that is better. Record your observations below.

LESSON
6

*DVD
and
discussion*

ORIGINS OF RADICAL LOVE (PART 2)

A Companion Study to *Battling Unbelief*, Session 6

LESSON OBJECTIVES

It is our prayer that after you have finished this lesson…

- You will see how the promise of future reward frees people to be sacrificially loving.

- You will follow the example of Jesus who endured suffering for the joy set before him.

- You will take practical steps to demonstrate your faith in future grace by engaging in loving acts of service to others.

Before You Watch the DVD, Study and Prepare

DAY 1—WHAT IS LOVE?

Question 1*: Give your own definition of love. Is love mainly an emotion or an act of the will? If possible, use Scripture in your answer.

Unconditional, voluntary, deep affection, feelings of goodwill, comes from God
1 Cor 13: 4-8   Love is patient, kind, doesn't envy or boast, is not rude or self-seeking, keeps no record of wrongs, rejoices with the truth, never fails
Romans 13:10 Love is the fulfillment of the law
1 Thes 3:12 - may God make your love overflow

Consider 1 Corinthians 13:3.

> ³ If I give away all I have, and if I deliver up my body to be burned, but have not love, I gain nothing.

Question 2: Is it possible to engage in a sacrificial act on behalf of another person and yet have that act not be loving? According to this verse, should we seek "gain" by having love?

It is possible to sacrificially serve another person without love when the gain sought is self-serving. We do seek gain in as much as joy of serving God is our gain.

DAY 2—GUESS WHO'S COMING TO DINNER

Read Luke 14:12–14.

> ¹² He said also to the man who had invited him, "When you give a dinner or a banquet, do not invite your friends or your brothers or your relatives or rich neighbors, lest they also invite you in return and you be repaid. ¹³ But when you give a feast, invite the poor, the crippled, the lame, the blind, ¹⁴ and you will be blessed, because they cannot repay you. You will be repaid at the resurrection of the just."

LESSON
7

DAY
2

LESSON 7

DAY 2

Question 3*: According to this passage, why should we invite the poor and weak to share meals with us? What is our motivation? Does this passage mean that we should never have friends and family over for dinner? Defend your answer.

Because they can't repay. Repayment at the resurrection of the just.

Study Matthew 13:44.

44 The kingdom of heaven is like treasure hidden in a field, which a man found and covered up. Then in his joy he goes and sells all that he has and buys that field.

Question 4: Why was this man able to sell all of his possessions "in his joy"? Is this an example of faith in future grace?

It was aware of the treasure.

DAY 3—SELL YOUR POSSESSIONS

Examine Luke 12:32–34.

32 Fear not, little flock, for it is your Father's good pleasure to give you the kingdom. 33 Sell your possessions, and give to the needy. Provide yourselves with moneybags that do not grow old, with a treasure in the heavens that does not fail, where no thief approaches and no moth destroys. 34 For where your treasure is, there will your heart be also.

Question 5*: Give three ways that God is described in this passage. If you had to clarify the logical connection between verse 32 and verse 33, what word(s) would you insert? Why did you discern this connection?

1. Shepherd, 2. Father 3. King

Therefore

Cause & effect

Question 6: Does verse 33 mean that all Christians should give all of their money to the poor? Defend your answer.

It doesn't say sell all your possessions, but we should strike a balance and use of our wealth provide for others

DAY 4—HOW SHOULD WE RESPOND TO PERSECUTION?

Question 7: How do most Christians respond when someone takes their property, power, or prestige? What actions do they normally take? How have you responded in the past?

Get angry & seek justice or revenge

LESSON
7

DAY
4

LESSON

7

DAY

5

Think on Hebrews 10:32–34.

32 But recall the former days when, after you were enlightened, you endured a hard struggle with sufferings, 33 sometimes being publicly exposed to reproach and affliction, and sometimes being partners with those so treated. 34 For you had compassion on those in prison, and you joyfully accepted the plundering of your property, since you knew that you yourselves had a better possession and an abiding one.

Question 8*: How did these Christians respond to their persecution and loss of property? What led them to respond in this way?

They endured and had compassion & joyfully accepted it

Because they knew they had a better possession and an abiding one (salvation in Christ & future reward)

DAY 5—LOOKING TO JESUS

Study Hebrews 12:1–2.

1 Therefore, since we are surrounded by so great a cloud of witnesses, let us also lay aside every weight, and sin which clings so closely, and let us run with endurance the race that is set before us, 2 looking to Jesus, the founder and perfecter of our faith, who for the joy that was set before him endured the cross, despising the shame, and is seated at the right hand of the throne of God.

Question 9*: How did Jesus endure the cross? What was "the joy that was set before him"?

By looking at the joy that was set before him. As, salvation & his sitting at the Father's right hand.

Question 10: Does the fact that Jesus endured the cross for the joy that was set before him make him less loving toward us? Why or why not?

No,

FURTHER UP AND FURTHER IN

Read Luke 17:5–10.

> [5] The apostles said to the Lord, "Increase our faith!" [6] And the Lord said, "If you had faith like a grain of mustard seed, you could say to this mulberry tree, 'Be uprooted and planted in the sea,' and it would obey you. [7] Will any one of you who has a servant plowing or keeping sheep say to him when he has come in from the field, 'Come at once and recline at table'? [8] Will he not rather say to him, 'Prepare supper for me, and dress properly, and serve me while I eat and drink, and afterward you will eat and drink'? [9] Does he thank the servant because he did what was commanded? [10] So you also, when you have done all that you were commanded, say, 'We are unworthy servants; we have only done what was our duty.'"

LESSON

7

Further up and further in

Question 11: In this passage, how does Jesus seek to increase the faith of his disciples? What is the main point of the story about the master and the servant?

The point is that we shouldn't be asking for faith we should be serving God. Our faith is increased through us knowing we are unworthy to be called children of God.

Question 12: Read Luke 17:10. How does this verse highlight the grace of God toward us?

Nothing we do will ever make us worthy of a relationship with God. It is only his gift of grace through Jesus Christ that this can happen.

Meditate on Hebrews 13:12–14.

12 So Jesus also suffered outside the gate in order to sanctify the people through his own blood. 13 Therefore let us go to him outside the camp and bear the reproach he endured. 14 For here we have no lasting city, but we seek the city that is to come.

Question 13: What does it mean to "go to him outside the camp"? What would it look like to obey this command in your situation?

The discarded and the shamed are outside the gate. We have to be willing to face that to be with Jesus

Question 14: Should we take our children with us when we "go to him outside the camp"? Is it right to expose children to danger for the cause of Christ?

Question 15: Can you think of any remaining objections to the truth that Christians should pursue their own pleasure in their acts of love? Record your reflections below.

While You Watch the DVD, Take Notes

What key words does John Piper highlight in his discussion of Luke 12:32–33?

What caused Moses to reject the fleeting pleasures of Egypt?

What causes John Piper to get "bent out of shape"?

What personal example does John Piper give for how he and his family "went outside the camp"?

LESSON

7

DVD
and
discussion

After You Watch the DVD, Discuss What You've Learned

1. Should all Christians sell their possessions and give all of their money to the poor? Defend your answer.

2. Discuss the difference between the way that many modern Christians respond to persecution and loss of property and power and the way that Christians in the first century responded. What accounts for the difference?

3. What is the most important new truth that you have learned about love from the past two lessons?

After You Discuss, Make Application

1. What was the most meaningful part of this lesson for you? Was there a sentence, concept, or idea that really struck you? Why? Record your thoughts in the space below.

2. Think and pray about specific ways that you could begin to obey Jesus' commands in Luke 14:32–34. Record your reflections below.

BATTLING THE UNBELIEF OF ANXIETY

A Companion Study to *Battling Unbelief*, Session 7

Sinsthtgehn the way of love

LESSON OBJECTIVES

It is our prayer that after you have finished this lesson…

- You will recognize that anxiety flows from unbelief in God and his promises.

- You will be able to identify different types of anxiety.

- You will begin to wage war against anxiety by trusting in the promises of God.

Before You Watch the DVD, Study and Prepare

DAY 1—DEFINING ANXIETY

The loss of confidence & security in God to [handwritten]
feelings of uneasiness that something bad is going to happen [handwritten]

LESSON 8

DAY 1

Question 1: Define anxiety in your own words. Give examples of things that make you feel anxious. Is it right to call anxiety a sin? Why or why not?

Being worried about the way something may turn out. [handwritten]
Anxiety is a sin because it shows we don't trust in the sovereignty of God [handwritten]
When you hold on to it; Fine line between worry & concern. [handwritten]
It may depend on what you do during times of worry. [handwritten]

Question 2*: Describe how you currently deal with anxiety. What steps do you take when you begin to feel anxious? What strategies do you use in this battle?

I used to not think about what made me anxious. I try to pray. [handwritten]

DAY 2—JESUS AGAINST ANXIETY

Read Matthew 6:25–34.

25 Therefore I tell you, do not be anxious about your life, what you will eat or what you will drink, nor about your body, what you will put on. Is not life more than food, and the body more than clothing? 26 Look at the birds of the air: they neither sow nor reap nor gather into barns, and yet your heavenly Father feeds them. Are you not of more value than they? 27 And which of you by being anxious can add a single

Crisis situations "I dont think I can make it - God will help you make it day by day.

hour to his span of life? 28 And why are you anxious about clothing? Consider the lilies of the field, how they grow: they neither toil nor spin, 29 yet I tell you, even Solomon in all his glory was not arrayed like one of these. 30 But if God so clothes the grass of the field, which today is alive and tomorrow is thrown into the oven, will he not much more clothe you, O you of little faith? 31 Therefore do not be anxious, saying, "What shall we eat?" or "What shall we drink?" or "What shall we wear?" 32 For the Gentiles seek after all these things, and your heavenly Father knows that you need them all. 33 But seek first the kingdom of God and his righteousness, and all these things will be added to you. 34 Therefore do not be anxious about tomorrow, for tomorrow will be anxious for itself. Sufficient for the day is its own trouble. → Lamentations 3 -

There is a perfect balance between troubles you will face today and God's mercy upon you each day. God's mercies are new every day.

Question 3: Rephrase this passage in your own words. What is the main point of this passage? Underline phrases that express this main point.

God is sovereign and he loves us, so we should not worry because he will take care of us. And worrying accomplishes nothing

Question 4*: This passage gives numerous reasons why we shouldn't worry. List at least five of these reasons and explain why they are helpful in the fight against anxiety.

1) Life is more than what we worry about - we shouldn't sweat the small stuff, and its all small stuff compared to eternity
2) Father takes care of our needs -

3) We are valuable in God's eyes

4) Worrying doesn't accomplish anything

5) God knows what our needs are

LESSON
8

DAY
2

Specific promises for specific folts of sin.

DAY 3—EASING ANXIETY ABOUT
USELESSNESS AND SUFFERING

LESSON
8

DAY
3

Study Isaiah 55:9–1.

9 For as the heavens are higher than the earth, so are my ways higher than your ways and my thoughts than your thoughts. 10 For as the rain and the snow come down from heaven and do not return there but water the earth, making it bring forth and sprout, giving seed to the sower and bread to the eater, 11 so shall my word be that goes out from my mouth; it shall not return to me empty, but it shall accomplish that which I purpose, and shall succeed in the thing for which I sent it.

Now study 1 Corinthians 15:58.

58 Therefore, my beloved brothers, be steadfast, immovable, always abounding in the work of the Lord, knowing that in the Lord your labor is not in vain. *in the Lord*

Question 5: According to these verses, where does confidence in the fruitfulness of our ministry come from? What analogy does Isaiah give in order to help us understand this? How could these verses be used when we are worried that we are being ineffective in ministry?

That God will accomplish his purpose (sometimes in spite of us)

Rain & snow come down and don't return without watering the earth

Know that our labor is not in vain.

2 Cor 12:9-10 - when I am weak Christ is strong in me

Investigate Romans 5:3–5.

> 3 More than that, we rejoice in our sufferings, knowing that suffering produces endurance, 4 and endurance produces character, and character produces hope, 5 and hope does not put us to shame, because God's love has been poured into our hearts through the Holy Spirit who has been given to us.

Question 6*: At times, many people feel anxious about enduring suffering. How does this passage enable us to fight anxiety about suffering? Give at least three truths from this passage that aid us in overcoming anxiety about suffering.

1. Suffering produces endurance which leads to hope
2. Paul was able to rejoice in his sufferings
3. God's love in our hearts gives us confidence in our hope.

DAY 4—GOD IS FOR US

Consider Romans 8:31.

> 31 What then shall we say to these things? If God is for us, who can be against us? (successfully nobody)

Question 7*: This verse is an example of a rhetorical question. Restate this rhetorical question in the form of a statement. Does this verse mean that no one will ever oppose us if God is on our side? Why or why not?

Since God is for us, no one can stand against us & ultimately be successful. Anyone can oppose us, ultimately though they are opposing God & will fail.

LESSON
8

DAY
4

Question 8: All of us recognize that many people are against us, even after we become Christians. Satan is against us. The world can be against us. Other people can be against us. So, if there are still many people against us after we become Christians, then how does this verse help us to overcome anxiety about opposition?

Because God is sovereign, and he is for us, so his will, which by definition will be accomplished, will accomplish good for us

Paul says, "If God is for us, who is against us?" Our first response to this question is: lots of people are against us! In fact, Jesus said, "You will be delivered up even by parents and brothers and relatives and friends, and they will put some of you to death and you will be hated by all on account of My name" (Luke 21:16–17). That's a lot of opposition. Paul knew that. Just a few verses later in this chapter he said, "For Thy sake we are being put to death all day long" (Romans 8:36).

What then did Paul mean when he said, "If God is for us, who is against us?" I think he meant, "Who can be *successfully* against us?" What opposition could there ever be against us that almighty God could not transform into our benefit? And the answer is: none.[25]

Psalm 34:19 - many are the afflictions of the righteous, but the Lord will deliver them from them all

Rom 5:35 - tribulations bring about perseverance. Faith is like a muscle; it doesn't test perseverance, it creates it

Rom. 14: 7-9 - whether we live or die, we are the Lord's

DAY 5—COMFORT ON THE DEATHBED

Question 9*: Imagine that you have been called to the hospital because a close friend only has a short while to live. This person is a Christian, but they are still anxious about death. How would you comfort your friend? What Scripture would you use? What prayer would you pray?   *Hebrews 13:5 , ~~Romans 8~~, Psalm 48*

Revelation 21 - "New Jerusalem"   Psalm 116 (esp. vs 15)

Romans 6: 22-23 you have been set free from sin and the result is eternal life

1 Cor 15: 50-57 - where o Death is your victory.

Romans 8:35-39

Read Hebrews 2:14–15.   *The world tends to medicate, but that anxiety can be used by God to help to focus on him*

> [14] Since therefore the children share in flesh and blood, he himself likewise partook of the same things, that through death he might destroy the one who has the power of death, that is, the devil, [15] and deliver all those who through fear of death were subject to lifelong slavery.

Now read 1 Corinthians 15:55–57.

> [55] "O death, where is your victory? O death, where is your sting?" [56] The sting of death is sin, and the power of sin is the law. [57] But thanks be to God, who gives us the victory through our Lord Jesus Christ.

Question 10: How does fear of death subject us to lifelong slavery? How do these verses comfort us in the face of death? What has happened to "death's victory" and "death's sting"?

It robs us of our joy, our confidence to proclaim Christ
It is all through the Bible that eternal life is ours
and that nothing will separate us from the love of God
It has been crucified with Christ on the cross

LESSON
8

DAY
5

FURTHER UP AND FURTHER IN

Study Romans 8:35–39.

35 Who shall separate us from the love of Christ? Shall tribulation, or distress, or persecution, or famine, or nakedness, or danger, or sword? 36 As it is written, "For your sake we are being killed all the day long; we are regarded as sheep to be slaughtered." 37 No, in all these things we are more than conquerors through him who loved us. 38 For I am sure that neither death nor life, nor angels nor rulers, nor things present nor things to come, nor powers, 39 nor height nor depth, nor anything else in all creation, will be able to separate us from the love of God in Christ Jesus our Lord.

Question 11: In this passage, what are the enemies and what is their goal? In light of this, what would it mean to "conquer" these foes? What does it mean to "more-than-conquer" them? What is the difference between conquering something and more-than-conquering something?

Enemies - forces of darkness ; Goal is to bring us tribulation, distress, persecution, etc. to separate us from God.

If you venture some act of obedience that magnifies the supreme value of Jesus Christ and get attacked by one of the enemies mentioned in verse 35, say famine or sword, what must happen for you to be called simply "a conqueror"? Answer: You must not be separated from the love of Jesus Christ. The aim of the attacker is to destroy you, and cut you off from Christ, and bring you to final ruin without God. You are a conqueror if you defeat this aim and remain in the love of Christ. God has promised that this will happen. Trusting this, we risk.

> But what must happen in this conflict with famine and sword if you are to be called more than a conqueror? One biblical answer is that a conqueror defeats his enemy, but one who is more than a conqueror subjugates his enemy. A conqueror nullifies the purpose of his enemy; one who is more than a conqueror makes the enemy serve his own purposes. A conqueror strikes down his foe; one who is more than a conqueror makes his foe his slave.[26]

Question 12: In light of the explanation above, what would it mean to more-than-conquer anxiety? How could you subjugate anxiety such that it serves your own purposes?

Use it as a barometer that something is not right

Many of us often feel anxious about big decisions that we have to make. We fear that we will make a wrong decision and we will stray from the path that God desires for us. Anxiety about such decisions often prevents us from making any decision at all. Read Psalm 25:8–12.

[8] Good and upright is the LORD; therefore he instructs sinners in the way. [9] He leads the humble in what is right, and teaches the humble his way. [10] All the paths of the LORD are steadfast love and faithfulness, for those who keep his covenant and his testimonies. [11] For your name's sake, O LORD, pardon my guilt, for it is great. [12] Who is the man who fears the LORD? Him will he instruct in the way that he should choose.

LESSON
8

Further up and further in

Question 13: From this passage, list the qualifications that must be met if God is to lead us and instruct us. Does our sin disqualify us from God's guidance? How do you know? How could this passage help someone who feels that God would never help them because their sin is too great?

We must be humble & sinners.

Psalm 32:8 - God will counsel & instruct us.

Study Jeremiah 32:40.

⁴⁰ I will make with them an everlasting covenant, that <u>I will</u> <u>not turn away from doing good to them</u>. And I will put the fear of me in their hearts, that <u>they may not turn from me</u>.

Question 14: This verse contains two purpose statements. Underline them. (Hint: they both begin with the word "that.") What two things has God committed to do in order to ensure that these purposes come to pass? How does this verse combat anxiety about whether or not you will persevere in faith?

He has made an everlasting covenant & put the fear of him in their hearts. God has made a covenant with us and he will keep it.

Question 15: One reason that it is so crucial to defeat the unbelief of anxiety is that anxiety often gives rise to many other sinful states of mind. Think for a moment about other sins that flow from anxiety. Make a list of these sins and how anxiety helps to produce them.

While You Watch the DVD, Take Notes

What is John Piper's definition of anxiety?

Summarize the conclusion that John Piper draws from comparing Matthew 6:34 to Lamentations 3:22–23.

What two qualifications are necessary if we are to receive God's counsel?

What analogy does John Piper use to explain the relationship between tribulation and perseverance?

What verse does John Piper use to comfort people on their deathbed?

After You Watch the DVD, Discuss What You've Learned

1. Discuss the importance of confronting today's problems with today's grace. Using Matthew 6:34 and Lamentations 3:22–23, show why it is unhelpful to worry about tomorrow's troubles.

2. In his discussion of Psalm 32:8, John Piper distinguishes between being delivered "from" afflictions and being delivered "out of" afflictions. What is the difference and why is it so crucial? What do you think "deliverance" means in this verse?

3. In his discussion of anxiety over perseverance in faith, John Piper asked the question "How do you know that you will wake up a Christian tomorrow?" Do you agree with the answer that he gives? Is your confidence concerning your perseverance in your own free will or in God's promise?

LESSON
8

*DVD
and
discussion*

After You Discuss, Make Application

1. What was the most meaningful part of this lesson for you? Was there a sentence, concept, or idea that really struck you? Why? Record your thoughts in the space below.

2. Identify one area of your life that you feel anxious about. Memorize a Bible verse that addresses that anxiety. Let a friend know what verse you are memorizing and quote it to them in one week.

Battling Anxiety About Old Age

Isaiah 46:3-4 – the Lord will bear us to our gray years.

Anxiety About Being A Christian

Php. 1:6 – God began a good work in us

Hebrews 7:25 – he is able to save *forever*
Preach the fullness of the gospel to ourselves
Jesus is speaking on our behalf to the Father.
Jer. 32:40 (see pg 84) – what makes us think we will wake up tomorrow with the same faith as today. It isn't us, it isn't our free will.
For new Christians, they think they don't want to change the way they live. This verse says God will enable us.

BATTLING THE UNBELIEF OF COVETOUSNESS

A Companion Study to *Battling Unbelief*, Session 8

Herbakkuh - 3:17   I will rejoice though there
is no fig on the tree or food to eat

LESSON OBJECTIVES

It is our prayer that after you have finished this lesson…

- You will recognize covetousness in its many forms.

- You will understand how Philippians 4.13 directly addresses the issue of covetousness.

- You will begin to make war on covetousness in your life and family.

Before You Watch the DVD, Study and Prepare

We should be generous because God is generous and we want
to be like him.

LESSON 9

DAY 1

DAY 1—DEFINING COVETOUSNESS

Success at work
Be in better shape

Question 1: Define covetousness in your own words. What are some common things that you covet?

Envying something someone else has or that you don't have and desiring it more than God. "It betrays a loss of contentment & Satisfaction in him" (pg 23)

Question 2*: How do you fight against covetousness in your own life? If you have children, how do you seek to teach them not to covet?

Rely on Gods promise that he will give us good things. Focus on how blessed we are

DAY 2—BEING FREE FROM THE LOVE OF MONEY

Read Joshua 1:5.

⁵ No man shall be able to stand before you all the days of your life. Just as I was with Moses, so I will be with you. I will not leave you or forsake you.

Now look at Psalm 118:6.

⁶ The LORD is on my side; I will not fear. What can man do to me?

Question 3*: What do these verses have to do with covetousness and greed? What is the common theme between them?

If our covetousness or greed is out of fear of not getting what we want or need, both these verses say God is on our side & he will be with us always

Examine Hebrews 13:5–6.

> [5] Keep your life free from love of money, and be content with what you have, for he has said, "I will never leave you nor forsake you." [6] So we can confidently say, "The Lord is my helper; I will not fear; what can man do to me?"

Question 4: How does the author to the Hebrews use these texts in relation to covetousness and greed? How do the Old Testament texts ground the exhortation to "be content with what you have"? Explain the logic of this passage.

It relates love of money and lack of contentment with fear and lack of understanding that God is with us.

If we are tempted to love money, we are to call to mind that God will never leave us

DAY 3—I CAN DO ALL THINGS

Consider Philippians 4:19.

> [19] And my God will supply every need of yours according to his riches in glory in Christ Jesus.

Question 5: Does the fact that God will supply all of our needs mean that Christians will never face hunger or suffer need? Why or why not?

No, but we are to be content with what we have and confident in the fact that God is with us.

All our needs to do what God has want us to do, it could be he wants us to die or work in the inner city, etc.

LESSON
9

DAY
3

Consider Philippians 4:13.

13 I can do all things through him who strengthens me.

Question 6*: This is one of the most oft-quoted verses in the Bible. Without looking in your Bible, describe the context in which this verse appears. What is included in the "all things" of this verse? Make a list.

Paul was thanking the Philippians for supporting him, but it had been a while and he knew what it was like to have plenty and to be in want. All things are those things that are pleasing to God—facing every circumstance—plenty & hunger, abundance & need.

DAY 4—THE SNARE OF MONEY

Now study Philippians 4:10–19.

10 I rejoiced in the Lord greatly that now at length you have revived your concern for me. You were indeed concerned for me, but you had no opportunity. 11 Not that I am speaking of being in need, for I have learned in whatever situation I am to be content. 12 I know how to be brought low, and I know how to abound. In any and every circumstance, I have learned the secret of facing plenty and hunger, abundance and need. 13 I can do all things through him who strengthens me. 14 Yet it was kind of you to share my trouble. 15 And you Philippians yourselves know that in the beginning of the gospel, when I left Macedonia, no church entered into partnership with me in giving and receiving, except you only. 16 Even in Thessalonica you sent me help for my needs once and again. 17 Not that I seek the gift, but I seek the fruit that

increases to your credit. [18] I have received full payment, and more. I am well supplied, having received from Epaphroditus the gifts you sent, a fragrant offering, a sacrifice acceptable and pleasing to God. [19] And my God will supply every need of yours according to his riches in glory in Christ Jesus.

Question 7: In context, what is Philippians 4:13 talking about? If facing hunger and need are some of the things that we are to endure, how does this affect the interpretation of Philippians 4:19?

→ Facing every circumstance.

When we read 4:13, we think of triumphs - but should the things it mentions is survive losses. I can suffer hunger, I can be brought low. I can do this because God will strengthen me. Whatever God calls us to do, we will be able to do.

Study 1 Timothy 6:6–11.

[6] Now there is great gain in godliness with contentment, [7] for we brought nothing into the world, and we cannot take anything out of the world. [8] But if we have food and clothing, with these we will be content. [9] But those who desire to be rich fall into temptation, into a snare, into many senseless and harmful desires that plunge people into ruin and destruction. [10] For the love of money is a root of all kinds of evils. It is through this craving that some have wandered away from the faith and pierced themselves with many pangs. [11] But as for you, O man of God, flee these things. Pursue righteousness, godliness, faith, love, steadfastness, gentleness.

LESSON
9

DAY
3

Question 8*: How does this passage help us to battle against covetousness? Underline all of the reasons why we should avoid the love of money and be content with what we have. How do those who desire to be rich fall into a snare? What alternative does Paul give to the love of money?

Knowing there is great godliness in being content. Money becomes their idol. Paul's alternative is to flee and pursue righteousness, godliness, faith, love, steadfastness, and gentleness.

DAY 5—HEARING THE WORD
AND DESIRING OTHER THINGS

In one of his parables, Jesus told about four different kinds of soils that receive seed. He then explained the parable to his disciples, comparing the soil to four different kinds of hearts and the seed to the word of God.

Read Mark 4:18–19.

18 And others are the ones sown among thorns. They are those who hear the word, 19 but the cares of the world and the deceitfulness of riches and the desires for other things enter in and choke the word, and it proves unfruitful.

Question 9: How does covetousness affect our understanding of Scripture? Describe a time in your life when a desire for other things choked the word.

The world competes for our time & energy. The more we invest in things it considers important, the less we will be abiding in the word of God.

Question 10*: Reflect on the things that you do and think each day. What sorts of things dominate your thoughts? What activities do you spend a lot of time doing? In light of your reflections, describe the inclination of your heart. What do your actions and thoughts reveal about the direction toward which your heart leans?

Work
Plans for the day } *busyness*
Working out   }

FURTHER UP AND FURTHER IN

> Have you ever considered that the Ten Commandments begin and end with virtually the same commandment—"You shall have no other gods before me" (Exodus 20:3) and "You shall not covet" (Exodus 20:17)? These are almost equivalent commands. Coveting is desiring anything other than God in a way that betrays a loss of contentment and satisfaction in Him. Covetousness is a heart divided between two gods.[27]

Question 11: According to John Piper, what is the relationship between covetousness and idolatry? Do you agree or disagree with his assessment? Can you think of any Scriptures that would support your position?

Whatever we covet, if its not God, that is our idol(s)

Col. 3:5 - covetousness amounts to idolatry

LESSON
9

Further up and further in

In his book *Future Grace*, John Piper says the following:

> When Paul says, "The love of money is the root of all evils"
> (1 Timothy 6:10, RSV), he means that the kind of heart that
> finds contentment in money and not in God is the kind of
> heart that produces all other kinds of evils...Covetousness
> is a breeding ground for a thousand other sins.

Question 12: Make a list of other sins that are rooted in covetousness. Describe how a covetous heart produces these other sins.

Greed
Theft   } a covetous heart will apply our resources to
Selfishness } acquiring our idols rather than serving God

Question 13: How does faith in future grace combat the list of sins which you made in Question 12?

Knowing that God has promised us riches far greater
than anything that could tempt us here should encourage us to
seek first his kingdom

Question 14: Do the biblical prohibitions against coveting imply that Christians should all take a vow of poverty? Why is a vow of poverty insufficient to kill the sin of covetousness?

God may chose to bless us with prosperity, but we need to be
generous with our wealth and guard against acquiring wealth
becoming our goal.

> God is not glorified when we keep for ourselves (no matter
> how thankfully) what we ought to be using to alleviate the
> misery of unevangelized, uneducated, unmedicated, and
> unfed millions. The evidence that many professing
> Christians have been deceived by this doctrine is how little
> they give and how much they own. God has prospered
> them. And by an almost irresistible law of consumer culture
> (baptized by a doctrine of health, wealth, and prosperity)
> they have bought bigger (and more) houses, newer (and
> more) cars, fancier (and more) clothes, better (and more)
> meat, and all manner of trinkets and gadgets and containers
> and devices and equipment to make life more fun.[28]

Question 15: Do you agree with John Piper's assessment of American consumerism? Do you see evidence of this mentality in your own life? If so, describe it. If not, describe how you have managed to counteract it.

While You Watch the DVD, Take Notes

What is John Piper's definition of covetousness? Desiring something not in God's glory

Is covetousness idolatry? What texts support this? Col 3:5 & Rom 2:?

Where do most people go wrong in their interpretation of Philippians 4:13?

What crucial truth about spiritual prayer is revealed in Psalm 119:36? Don't pray for stuff - our health, safety or trip, food, things go well we can pray for this, but we most importantly should be praying for our heart, our inclinations should be toward God

LESSON

9

DVD and discussion

After You Watch the DVD, Discuss What You've Learned

1. In this session, John Piper noted that covetousness is a huge issue for Americans. Discuss how you see the sin of covetousness manifested in your own life, in your family, and in society.

2. How does John Piper's interpretation of Philippians 4:13 compare to the way you have understood this text in the past? Do you agree with his interpretation? Why or why not?

3. What is the difference between praying for material things and praying for spiritual things? How does Psalm 119:36 illustrate this? Is it wrong to pray for material things?

After You Discuss, Make Application

1. What was the most meaningful part of this lesson for you? Was there a sentence, concept, or idea that really struck you? Why? Record your thoughts in the space below.

2. Discuss Philippians 4:13 with a friend. Ask them what they think this verse means. Then share with them some of the insights that you learned in this lesson. Record important observations below.

BATTLING THE UNBELIEF OF LUST

A Companion Study to *Battling Unbelief*, Session 9

LESSON OBJECTIVES

It is our prayer that after you have finished this lesson…

- You will understand what is at stake in the war against lust.

- You will begin to take drastic action in order to sever the root of sexual sin.

- God will reveal himself to you in a new way such that you are better able to make war against the passions of the flesh.

Before You Watch the DVD, Study and Prepare

DAY 1—DEFINING LUST

LESSON
10

DAY
1

Question 1: Define lust in your own words. Give examples of lust.

Going beyond an appreciation of something and attempting to make it mine ~~entire~~ in my mind ~~or forward~~. Realm of thought, imagination, and desire that leads to sexual misconduct. Pursuing illicit thoughts or images with ~~mind~~ with arrow to stimulate sexual

Question 2*: Describe your strategy in the war against sexual sin. Give your foundational goals and your practical methods of avoiding lust. Give examples of strategies that have not helped you in the past.

Foundational goal is to not want to pursue sexual sin, to make it distasteful to me as it is to God. Practical methods: maintaining intimacy with wife; avoid opportunities

DAY 2—WHAT'S AT STAKE IN
THE BATTLE WITH LUST

Read Matthew 5:27–30.

27 You have heard that it was said, "You shall not commit adultery." 28 But I say to you that everyone who looks at a woman with lustful intent has already committed adultery with her in his heart. 29 If your right eye causes you to sin, tear it out and throw it away. For it is better that you lose one of your members than that your whole body be thrown into hell. 30 And if your right hand causes you to sin, cut it off and throw it away. For it is better that you lose one of your members than that your whole body go into hell.

Question 3*: In this passage, Jesus clarifies what is meant by the prohibition against adultery. How does Jesus define adultery? What prescription does Jesus give us in the battle against lust? What are the consequences of failing to take action against this sin?

Looking at a woman with lustful intent.

Cast away whatever is causing you to sin.

Whole body thrown in hell

Question 4: Should we take Matthew 5:29–30 literally? In other words, does Jesus command us to literally tear out our eye if we fall into sexual sin? Give reasons for your interpretation.

and to take drastic steps to do so

He wants us to remove from our lives the root causes of sin. He is not teaching self-mutilation, because even a blind man can lust. Suffer whatever you must to win the war with lust.

DAY 3—LUST AND THE TRIVIALITY OF LIFE

Examine 1 Thessalonians 4:3–5.

> ³ For this is the will of God, your sanctification: that you abstain from sexual immorality; ⁴ that each one of you know how to control his own body in holiness and honor, ⁵ not in the passion of lust like the Gentiles who do not know God;

Question 5: According to this passage, what is the relationship between knowing God and abstaining from sexual immorality? Why do you think that Paul describes abstaining from sexual immorality in terms of honor?

The Gentiles who don't know God allow passion of lust to control them.

Because our bodies are "temples" of God, which should be honored.

LESSON

10

DAY

3

My conviction is that one of the main reasons the world and the church are awash in lust and pornography (by men and women—30% of internet pornography is now viewed by women) is that our lives are intellectually and emotionally disconnected from infinite, soul-staggering grandeur for which we were made. Inside and outside the church western culture is drowning in a sea of triviality, pettiness, banality, and silliness. Television is trivial. Radio is trivial. Conversation is trivial. Education is trivial. Christian books are trivial. Worship styles are trivial. It is inevitable that the human heart, which was made to be staggered with the supremacy of Christ, but instead is drowning in a sea of banal entertainment, will reach for the best natural buzz that life can give: sex.

Therefore, the deepest cure to our pitiful addictions is not any mental strategies—and I believe in them and have my own (see ANTHEM[29]). The deepest cure is to be intellectually and emotionally staggered by the infinite, everlasting, unchanging supremacy of Christ in all things. This is what it means to *know* him. Christ has purchased this gift for us at the cost of his life. Therefore, I say again with Hosea, let us know, let us press on to know the Lord.[30]

Question 6*: Do you agree with John Piper's analysis of the root cause behind sexual sin? Does this analysis hold true in your own life? Explain your answer.

I agree that we are drowning in a sea of triviality I don't know that this is the cause behind sexual sin. It is a misplaced need for intimacy.

DAY 4—SEXUALITY AND BEING FULLY HUMAN

Question 7*: Suppose you met a single person who is seeking to justify their continued fornication. Their reasoning is that it is necessary for them to be sexually active in order to experience their full humanity. In other words, refraining from sexual activity would keep them from being fully human. How would you respond to such a person? Cite Scripture in your answer.

Sexuality was not made to experience humanity, but to know God better a means to be a pointer and foretaste of our relationship with him.
Eph. 4:22, 2 Peter 1:3-4, 2 Tim 2:22-26,

Question 8: What other areas of our lives are affected when we fall into sexual temptation? Give specific examples from your life. How can the loss of joy in these areas help us to make war on lust?

DAY 5—FIGHTING FIRE WITH FIRE

Question 9: On page 336 of *Future Grace*, John Piper says that he often tells young people that "they must fight fire with fire." What do you think he means by this statement in relation to the fight against sexual sin? What "fire" must we use to fight the "fire" of sexual temptation?

LESSON
10

DAY
5

Knowing Christ in the fullest Biblical sense of grasping great truth about Christ, growing in fellowship with him, and being satisfied with the supremacy of Christ.
See ANTHEM (pg 106) Attack the promise of sin with the promises of Christ

LESSON
10

DAY
5

In the fall of 1982, *Leadership* magazine carried an unsigned article by a pastor who confessed to years of bondage to pornography of the grossest kind. He tells the story of what finally released him. It is a resounding confirmation of what I am trying to say. The author ran across a book by Francois Mauriac, the Catholic French novelist, *What I Believe*. In it Mauriac admitted how the plague of guilt had not freed him from lust. He concludes that there is one powerful reason to seek purity, the one Christ gave in the Beatitudes: "Blessed are the pure in heart, for they shall see God" (Matthew 5:8). It is the "precious and magnificent" promise that the pure see God that empowers our escape from lust. The lust-bound pastor wrote,

> *The thought hit me like a bell rung in the dark, silent hall. So far, none of the scary, negative arguments against lust had succeeded in keeping me from it…But here was a description of what I was missing by continuing to harbor lust: I was limiting my own intimacy with God. The love he offers is so transcendent and possessing that it requires our faculties to be purified and cleansed before we can possibly contain it. Could he, in fact, substitute another thirst and another hunger for one I had never filled? Would Living Water somehow quench lust? That was the gamble of faith.[31]*

Question 10*: What was the great discovery that liberated this pastor from bondage to sexual sin? How is this an example of faith in future grace? How does this truth relate to the need to "fight fire with fire?"

His bondage was preventing him from seeing God. He had to have faith that seeing God was more important than his base cravings. He used the promise that the pure in heart will see God as his fire.

FURTHER UP AND FURTHER IN

Read John Piper's sermon, "Sex and the Supremacy of Christ, Part 1" at www.desiringgod.org/library/topics/sex/sex_supremacy_christ_pt1.html.

Question 11: According to John Piper, what is the ultimate reason that God made human beings sexual? What Scripture texts does he use to demonstrate his point?

As a way to know God more.

Ezekiel 16: 4-10 - God's free & undeserved mercy (covering Israel's nakedness)
13-33 - turning from God to foreign Gods (Israel whoring)
35-37 - God's judgement (lovers will be turned against her)
59-63 - God will remember his covenant

Question 12: What is the second of John Piper's main points in this sermon?

Knowing God in Christ serves to prevent misuse of our sexuality

All sexual corruption serves to conceal the true knowledge of Christ, and the true knowledge of Christ serves to prevent sexual corruption.

Read John Piper's sermon, "Sex and the Supremacy of Christ, Part 2" at www.desiringgod.org/library/sermons/04/092604.html.

Question 13: What was the most provocative part of this sermon to you? Why did this part stand out in your mind? Record your reflections below.

We must suffer in order to be sexually pure.

Knowing all that God promises to be for us in Christ both now and for endless ages with ever-increasing joy, frees us from the compulsion that we must avoid pain and maximize pleasure in this world.

LESSON

10

Further up and further in

Question 14: In this sermon, John Piper uses three analogies to describe how knowing and embracing the supremacy of Christ in all things relates to everything else in your life. What are the three analogies?

1) Planets of our life (sexuality, desires, commitments, beliefs,) orbiting around the immense sun of supremacy of Jesus Christ.

2) Tiny space ships of moral strategies trying to nudge the planets (sexuality) into orbit.

Question 15: In the space below, draw a picture that illustrates one of the three analogies that John Piper uses in this sermon. Be sure to label your illustration.

2. Ballast at the bottom of our little boat keeping it from being capsized by waves of sexual temptation.

3. Foundation that holds up the building of our lives so we can build with strategies of sexual purity.

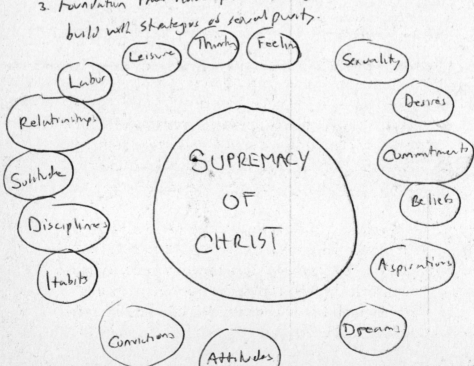

[handwritten top margin: Unforgiven lust will ~~distort~~ destroy the soul.]

While You Watch the DVD, Take Notes *[handwritten: Eph 4:22 - deceit]*

What is John Piper's definition of lust?

[handwritten: 1 Peter 1:14 - ignorance]

[handwritten: 1 Thes 4:4-5 - do not know God]

Lust grows out of _Suppressing_ _the knowledge_ of
God and his _promises_.

[handwritten: 2 Peter 1:3-4 - power for Godliness comes through knowledge of him]

What analogy does John Piper use to describe his philosophy in
combating lust? *[handwritten: Techniques are like cranes picky but up out of the mud of lust. Knowing God is like a rising tide which raises all the boats up at once.]*

How did John Piper respond to the single man who justified his fornication on the grounds that he wanted to experience his full
humanity? *[handwritten: Psalm 84:11 - no good thing does he withhold from those who walk uprightly]*

Be _killing_ sin or _it_ will be _killing_ you.

[handwritten: I know one person who was fully human (Jesus) and he never had sex]

After You Watch the DVD, Discuss What You've Learned

NOTE: Due to the sensitive nature of this material, we recommend that you divide
into gender-specific groups for this discussion.

1. Discuss the situation of the single man who justified his fornication by arguing for his need to experience his full
   humanity. Give the rationale for both sides of the argu-
   ment. Which do you find more persuasive?

2. In this session, John Piper describes the fight with lust
   in terms of boats which are sunk in the mud. He then
   gives two alternatives for how to get the boats out of the
   mud. Describe these two alternatives. Which method
   do you think is most common? Which method do you
   use most of the time?

LESSON
10

*DVD
and
discussion*

3. In your groups, make a list of everything that is at stake in the war against lust. Then make a list of strategies (both big-picture strategies and practical methods) that you could use to fight against lust.

After You Discuss, Make Application

1. What was the most meaningful part of this lesson for you? Was there a sentence, concept, or idea that really struck you? Why? Record your thoughts in the space below.

2. Jesus commanded us to cut out parts of our lives that cause us to stumble. Identify three sources of temptation in your life that lead you into sin. Share these three sources with a trusted friend or counselor. Take steps to cut these sources of temptation out of your life.

A - avoid as much as possible sights & situations that arouse unfitting desire.

N - say no to every lustful thought within 5 seconds.

T - turn the mind forcefully toward Christ as a superior satisfaction Attack the promise of sin with the promises of Christ

H - hold the promise and pleasure of Christ until it pushes other images out Fix our eyes on Jesus and hold it as long as it takes with God

E - enjoy a superior satisfaction, delight in Christ, plead for satisfaction in him

M - move away from idleness and vulnerable activities to a useful activity.

BATTLING THE UNBELIEF OF BITTERNESS AND IMPATIENCE

A Companion Study to *Battling Unbelief*, Session 10

LESSON OBJECTIVES

It is our prayer that after you have finished this lesson...

- You will see how bitterness and impatience both flow from a lack of faith.

- You will be freed from bitterness by trusting in the future justice of God.

- The sovereign goodness of God will begin to liberate you from any impatience in your life.

Before You Watch the DVD, Study and Prepare

DAY 1—DEFINING BITTERNESS

Question 1*: Define bitterness in your own words. Describe a situation in which you have harbored bitterness toward someone. What caused you to feel bitter toward them?

Resentment & ill-will toward someone or toward God

Question 2: Why is bitterness such a serious sin? How do you currently resist the impulse to be bitter against someone? How do you think faith in future grace helps to free us from bitterness?

It's the antithesis of the love we are called to have for others.

DAY 2—FOLLOWING IN THE STEPS OF JESUS

Look at 1 Peter 2:21–23.

> 21 For to this you have been called, because Christ also suffered for you, leaving you an example, so that you might follow in his steps. 22 He committed no sin, neither was deceit found in his mouth. 23 When he was reviled, he did not revile in return; when he suffered, he did not threaten, but continued entrusting himself to him who judges justly.

Question 3*: Underline the phrases that indicate how Jesus responded to injustice committed against him. What gave him the ability to endure such injustice? How can we emulate Jesus in this area?

He trusted God. Trust God that he will judge justly

Study Ephesians 4:31–32.

> [31] Let all bitterness and wrath and anger and clamor and slander be put away from you, along with all malice. [32] Be kind to one another, tenderhearted, forgiving one another, as God in Christ forgave you.

Question 4: According to this passage, why should we forgive other people? Does this verse mean that we should immediately trust those who have wronged us? Explain your answer.

Because God forgave us. We can forgive someone (i.e. release any debt they have to us) without trusting them. Trust has to be re-earned

DAY 3—FUTURE JUDGMENT AND FUTURE GRACE

LESSON

11

Ponder Romans 12:19.

> [19] Beloved, never avenge yourselves, but leave it to the wrath of God, for it is written, "Vengeance is mine, I will repay, says the Lord."

DAY

3

Question 5*: Explain the logic of this verse. How does the promise of future judgment ground the command to not avenge ourselves?

We need to trust that God will do what is best for us. If someone hurts us, he will take care of it

---

Is the judgment of God on our enemies an act of future grace toward us? This is a crucial question because the point of this book is to help people live by faith in future grace. But what I find in the New Testament is that one powerful way of overcoming bitterness and revenge is to have faith in the promise that God will settle accounts with our offenders so that we don't have to. The New Testament teaches that we are freed from vengeance by believing that God will take vengeance for us, if he must. So my question is this: Is believing in God's vengeance an example of faith in future *grace*, or is it only faith in future *justice*? My answer is that faith in God's judgment is another form of faith in future grace. Therefore living by faith in future grace involves overcoming vengeance and bitterness by trusting God to settle all our accounts justly.[32]

Question 6: Is it right to call faith in God's vengeance an example of faith in future grace? How does believing that God will settle all of your accounts justly enable you to overcome bitterness and a desire to avenge yourself?

DAY 4—DEFINING IMPATIENCE

Question 7*: Define impatience in your own words. Give examples of situations in which you have felt impatient. How are you currently seeking to overcome impatience in your life?

> God is ruling the world. He is ruling history. And it is all for the good of his people and the glory of his name. "From of old they have not heard nor perceived by ear, neither has the eye seen a God besides Thee, who *acts in behalf of the one who waits for Him*" (Isaiah 64:4). The power of patience flows through faith in the future, sovereign grace of God.[33]

Question 8: According to Isaiah 64:4, what distinguishes the true God from all other gods? How does faith in the sovereign grace of God enable us to be patient? Why is it important to trust in the *sovereignty* of God?

DAY 5—OBSERVING PATIENCE
IN THE LIFE OF JOSEPH

LESSON
11

DAY
5

The story of Joseph can be found in Genesis 37–50. It is a story filled with hardship and suffering. Read this story quickly and answer the following questions.

LESSON
11

DAY
5

Question 9*: Make a list of the hardships that Joseph had to endure. How many of these hardships were the result of the sin of others? How many were Joseph's fault? Why were all of these hardships tests of Joseph's patience?

Question 10: How did Joseph respond to each hardship that he faced? What sustained him through these trials? At the end of the story, how did Joseph view his sufferings? Cite Scripture in your answer.

FURTHER UP AND FURTHER IN

Question 11: In your mind, what is the difference between a desire for justice and a desire for vengeance? How do the two desires relate to each other?

What gives so much force to the impulse of anger...is the overwhelming sense that the offender does not *deserve* forgiveness. That is, the grievance is so deep and so justifiable that not only does self-righteousness strengthen our indignation, but so does a legitimate sense of moral outrage. It's the deep sense of legitimacy that gives our bitterness its unbending compulsion. We feel that a great crime would be committed if the magnitude of evil we've experienced were just dropped and we let bygones be bygones. We are torn: our moral sense says this evil cannot be ignored, and the Word of God says we must forgive.[34]

Question 12: Suppose that a friend of yours has been wronged so deeply that they feel the tension that John Piper describes in the paragraph above. How would you help them to resolve this tension? What truths would you highlight for them? How would your counsel be different if the person who wronged them was a Christian?

Question 13: How does past grace help us in the battle against bitterness? Describe how the cross of Christ enables us to kill the unbelief of bitterness and vengeance. Cite Scripture in your answer.

LESSON
11

*Further up
and
further in*

Examine James 5:7–11.

7 Be patient, therefore, brothers, until the coming of the Lord. See how the farmer waits for the precious fruit of the earth, being patient about it, until it receives the early and the late rains. 8 You also, be patient. Establish your hearts, for the coming of the Lord is at hand. 9 Do not grumble against one another, brothers, so that you may not be judged; behold, the Judge is standing at the door. 10 As an example of suffering and patience, brothers, take the prophets who spoke in the name of the Lord. 11 Behold, we consider those blessed who remained steadfast. You have heard of the steadfastness of Job, and you have seen the purpose of the Lord, how the Lord is compassionate and merciful.

Question 14: Underline all of the reasons that this passage gives for being patient. How does each one serve to strengthen patience in our hearts?

Read 2 Corinthians 4:16–18.

16 So we do not lose heart. Though our outer nature is wasting away, our inner nature is being renewed day by day. 17 For this slight momentary affliction is preparing for us an eternal weight of glory beyond all comparison, 18 as we look not to the things that are seen but to the things that are unseen. For the things that are seen are transient, but the things that are unseen are eternal.

Question 15: Look up 2 Corinthians 11:21–33 in your own Bible. According to this passage, what did Paul consider to be "slight momentary affliction"? What enabled Paul to endure such trials and hardships? How is this an example of patience?

While You Watch the DVD, Take Notes

What is John Piper's definition of bitterness?

All sins will be duly punished, either _____ or _____.

What is John Piper's definition of impatience?

According to John Piper, what is the key to overcoming impatience?

What modern person does John Piper give as an example of patience? Why does he use this person?

After You Watch the DVD, Discuss What You've Learned

1. How does the cross of Christ enable us to be outraged at injustice and yet still refrain from taking vengeance on those who have wronged us? How did the cross keep the moral structure of the universe intact?

LESSON
11

DVD and discussion

2. Discuss how faith in the vengeance of God liberates us from bitterness and grudges. Is trusting in the future vengeance of God really an example of faith in future grace?

3. Discuss the story of Joseph in Genesis 37–50. In light of this story, how should we view the various trials and tribulations that we endure? Is it right for us to say that God sent them into our lives? Why or why not?

After You Discuss, Make Application

1. What was the most meaningful part of this lesson for you? Was there a sentence, concept, or idea that really struck you? Why? Record your thoughts in the space below.

2. Think of a relationship that you have that is currently being strained by bitterness. If you have wronged the other person, seek out their forgiveness. If you have been wronged, begin to pray that God would liberate you from bitterness by trusting in his justice and grace.

REVIEW AND CONCLUSION

LESSON OBJECTIVES

It is our prayer that after you have finished this lesson…

- You will be able to summarize and synthesize what you've learned.

- You will hear what others in your group have learned.

- You will share with others how you have begun to battle against unbelief in your life.

WHAT HAVE YOU LEARNED?

There are no study questions to answer in preparation for this lesson. Instead, spend your time writing a few paragraphs that explain what you've learned in this group study. To help you do this, you may choose to review the notes you've taken in the previous lessons. Then, after you've written down what you've learned, write down some questions that still remain in your mind about anything addressed in these lessons. Be prepared to share these reflections and questions with the group in the next lesson.

NOTES

Use this space to record anything in the group discussion that you
want to remember:

LEADER'S GUIDE

As the leader of this group study, **it is imperative that you are completely familiar with this study guide** and with the *Battling Unbelief* DVD Set. Therefore, it is our strong recommendation (1) that you read and understand the introduction; (2) that you skim each lesson, surveying its layout and content; and (3) that you read the entire Leader's Guide *before* you begin the group study and distribute the study guides.

LEADING PRODUCTIVE DISCUSSIONS[36]

It is our conviction that the best group leaders foster an environment in their group which engages the participants. We learn by solving problems or by working through things that provoke curiosity or concern. This study guide is meant to facilitate an investigation into biblical truth—an investigation that is shared by the group leader and the participants. Therefore, we encourage you to adopt the posture of a "fellow-learner" who invites participation from everyone in the group.

It might surprise you how eager people can be to share what they have learned in preparing for each lesson. Therefore, you should invite participation by asking your group participants to share their discoveries. Here are some of our "tips" on facilitating discussion that is engaging and helpful:

- Don't be uncomfortable with silence initially. Once the first participant shares their response, others will be likely to join in. But if you cut the silence short by prompting them, then they are more likely to wait for you to prompt them every time.

- Affirm every answer, if possible, and draw out the participants by asking for clarification. Your aim is to make them feel comfortable sharing their ideas and learning, so be extremely hesitant to "shut down" someone's contribution or "trump" it with your own. This does not mean, however, that you shouldn't correct false ideas—just do it in a spirit of gentleness and love.

- Don't allow a single person, or a few persons, to dominate the discussion. Involve everyone, if possible, and intentionally invite participation from those who are more reserved or hesitant.

- Labor to show the significance of their study. Emphasize the things that the participants could not have learned without doing the homework.

- Avoid talking too much. The group leader should not monopolize the discussion, but rather guide and shape it. If the group leader does the majority of the talking, the participants will be less likely to interact and engage, and therefore they will not learn as much. Avoid constantly adding the "definitive last word."

- The group leader should feel the freedom to linger on a topic or question if the group demonstrates interest. The group leader should also pursue digressions that are helpful and relevant. There is a balance to this, however: The group leader *should* attempt to cover the material. So avoid the extreme of constantly wandering off topic, but also avoid the extreme of limiting the conversation in a way that squelches curiosity or learning.

- The group leader's passion, or lack thereof, is infectious. Therefore, if you demonstrate little enthusiasm for the material, it is almost inevitable that your participants will likewise be bored. But if you have a genuine excitement for what you are studying, and if you truly think Bible study is worthwhile, then your group will be impacted positively. Therefore, it is our recommendation that before you come to the group, you spend enough time working through the homework and praying, so that you can overflow with genuine enthusiasm for the Bible and for God in your group. This point cannot be stressed enough. Delight yourself in God and in his Word!

BEFORE LESSON 1

Before the first lesson, you will need to know approximately how many participants you will have in your group study. **Each participant will need their own study guide.** Therefore, be sure to order enough study guides. You will distribute these study guides at the beginning of the first lesson.

It is also our strong recommendation that you, as the leader, familiarize yourself with this study guide and the *Battling Unbelief* DVD Set in order to answer any questions that might arise, and also to ensure that each group session runs smoothly and maximizes the learning of the participants. It is not necessary for you to preview *Battling Unbelief* in its entirety—although it certainly wouldn't hurt—but you should be prepared to navigate your way through each DVD menu.

DURING LESSON 1

Each lesson is designed for a one-hour group session. Lessons 2–12 require preparatory work from the participant before this group session. Lesson 1, however, requires no preparation on the part of the participant.

The following schedule is how we suggest that you use the first hour of your group study:

Introduction to the Study Guide (10 min)
Introduce this study guide and the *Battling Unbelief* DVD set. Share with the group why you chose to lead the group study using these resources. Inform your group of the commitment that this study will require and motivate them to work hard. Pray for the twelve-week study, asking God for the grace you will need. Then distribute one study guide to each participant. You may read the introduction aloud, if you want, or you may immediately turn the group to Lesson 1 (starting on page 7 of this study guide).

Personal Introductions (15 min)

Since group discussion will be an integral part of this guided study, it is crucial that each participant feels welcome and safe. The goal of each lesson is for every participant to contribute to the discussion in some way. Therefore, during these 15 minutes, have each participant introduce themselves. You may choose to use the questions listed in the section entitled, "About Yourself," or you may ask questions of your own choosing.

Discussion (25 min)

Transition from the time of introductions to the discussion questions, listed under the heading, "A Preview of Battling Unbelief." Invite everyone in the class to respond to these questions, but don't let the discussion become too involved. These questions are designed to spark interest and generate questions.

Review and Closing (10 min)

End the group session by reviewing Lesson 2 with the group participants and informing them of the preparation that they must do before the group meets again. Encourage them to be faithful in preparing for the next lesson. Answer any questions that the group may have, and then close in prayer.

BEFORE LESSONS 2–11

As the group leader, you should do all the preparation for each lesson that is required of the group participants, that is, the ten study questions. Furthermore, it is highly recommended that you complete the entire "Further Up and Further In" section. This is not required of the group participants, but it will enrich your preparation and help you to guide and shape the conversation more effectively.

The group leader should also preview the session of *Battling Unbelief* that will be covered in the next lesson. So, for example, if the group participants are doing the preparatory work for Lesson 3, you should pre-view *Battling Unbelief*, Session 2, before the group meets and views it. Previewing each session will better equip you to understand the material and answer questions. If you want to pause the DVD in the midst of the session in order to clarify or discuss, previewing the session will allow you to plan where you want to take your pauses.

Finally, you may want to supplement or modify the discussion questions or the application assignment. Please remember that this study guide is a resource; any additions or changes you make that bet-ter match the study to your particular group are encouraged. This study guide should function as a helpful tool and *resource*. As the group leader, your own discernment, creativity, and guidance are invaluable, and you should adapt the material as you see fit.

Plan for about two hours of your own preparation before each lesson.

DURING LESSONS 2–11

Again, let us stress that during Lessons 2–9, you may use the group time in whatever way you desire. The following schedule, however, is what we suggest:

Discussion (10 min)
Begin your time with prayer. The tone you set in your prayer will likely be impressed upon the group participants: if your prayer is serious and heart-felt, the group participants will be serious about prayer; if your prayer is hasty, sloppy, or a token gesture, the group participants will share this same attitude toward prayer. So model the kind of praying that you desire your students to imitate. Remember, the blood of Jesus has bought your access to the throne of grace.

After praying, review the preparatory work that the participants completed. How did they answer the questions? Which questions did they find to be the most interesting or the most confusing? What observations or insights can they share with the group? If you would like to review some tips for leading productive discussion, please turn to the appendix at the end of this Leader's Guide.

The group participants will be provided an opportunity to apply what they've learned in Lessons 2–9. As the group leader, you can choose whether it would be appropriate for the group to discuss these assignments during this ten-minute time slot.

DVD Viewing (30 min)[35]

Play the session for *Battling Unbelief* that corresponds to the lesson you are studying. You may choose to pause the DVD at crucial points to check for understanding and provide clarification. Or, you may choose to watch the DVD without interruption.

Discussion and Closing (20 min)

Facilitate discussion on what was taught during John Piper's session. You may do this by first reviewing the DVD notes (under the heading, "While You Watch the DVD, Take Notes"), and then proceeding to the discussion questions listed under the heading, "After You Watch the DVD, Discuss What You've Learned." These discussion questions are meant to be springboards that launch the group into further and deeper discussion. Don't feel constrained to these questions if the group discussion begins to move in other helpful directions.

Close the time by briefly reviewing the application section and the homework that is expected for the next lesson. Pray and dismiss.

NOTE: The *Battling Unbelief* DVD set contains an appendix which provides a helpful review of the first four DVD sessions. If at any point your group is struggling with concepts from these first sessions, it might be helpful to watch this 15 minute clip in order to clarify the main points. There are no discussion questions for this appendix.

BEFORE LESSON 12

It is important that you encourage the group participants to complete the preparatory work for Lesson 12. This assignment invites the participant to reflect on what they've learned and what remaining questions they still have. As the group leader, this would be a helpful assignment for you to complete as well. In addition, you may want to write down the key concepts of this DVD series that you want the group participants to walk away with.

DURING LESSON 12

The group participants are expected to complete a reflection exercise as part of their preparation for Lesson 12. The bulk of the group time during this last lesson should be focused on reviewing and synthesizing what was learned. Encourage each participant to share some of their recorded thoughts. Attempt to answer any remaining questions that they might have.

To close this last lesson, you might want to spend extended time in prayer. If appropriate, take prayer requests relating to what the participants have learned in these ten weeks, and bring these requests to God.

It would be completely appropriate for you, the group leader, to give a final charge or word of exhortation to end this group study. Speak from your heart and out of the overflow of joy that you have in God.

Please receive our blessing for all you group leaders who choose to use this study guide:

> The LORD bless you and keep you; the LORD make his
> face to shine upon you and be gracious to you; the
> LORD lift up his countenance upon you and give you
> peace. (Numbers 6:24–26)

SIX-SESSION INTENSIVE OPTION

We understand that there are circumstances which may prohibit a group from devoting twelve sessions to this study. In view of this, we have designed a six-session intensive option for groups that need to complete the material in less time. In the intensive option, the group should meet for two hours each week. Here is our suggestion for how to complete the material in six weeks:

Week 1   Introduction to the Study Guide and Lesson 1
Week 2   Lessons 2 and 3 (DVD Sessions 1 and 2)
Week 3   Lessons 4 and 5 (DVD Sessions 3 and 4)
Week 4   Lessons 6 and 7 (DVD Sessions 5 and 6)
Week 5   Lessons 8 and 9 (DVD Sessions 7 and 8)
Week 6   Lessons 10 and 11 (DVD Sessions 9 and 10)

Notice that we have not included Lesson 12 in the intensive option. Moreover, because each participant is required to complete two lessons per week, it will be necessary to combine the number of "days" within each lesson so that all of the material is covered. Thus, for example, during Week 2 in the intensive option, each participant should complete

- Lesson 2, Days 1 and 2, on the first day;

- Lesson 2, Days 3 and 4, on the second day;

- Lesson 2, Day 5 and Lesson 3, Day 1, on the third day;

- Lesson 3, Days 2 and 3, on the fourth day;

- and Lesson 3, Days 4 and 5, on the fifth day.

Because of the amount of material, we recommend that students focus on questions marked with an asterisk (*) first, and then, if time permits, complete the rest of the questions.

NOTES

1. All Scripture is cited from the *English Standard Version* (ESV).
2. While this study guide is designed for a twelve-session study, it is possible to complete it in six sessions. For instructions on how to use this study guide for a six-session group study, turn to Appendix A: Six-Session Intensive Option.
3. Although this resource is designed to be used in a group setting, it can also be used by the independent learner. Such a learner would have to decide for themselves how to use this resource in the most beneficial way. We would suggest doing everything but the group discussion, if possible.
4. Questions marked with an asterisk (*) are questions that we deem to be particularly significant. If your group is completing this study using the six-session intensive option, we recommend that you complete these questions first, and then, if time permits, complete the remaining questions. For more information, see Appendix A—Six-Session Intensive Option.
5. Excerpt taken from *Desiring God* (Sisters, Oregon: Multnomah Publishers, 2003), 41–42.
6. Thought #425, quoted by John Piper in *Desiring God*, 19.
7. Excerpt taken from a sermon at www.desiringgod.org/library/topics/edwards/edwards_mind.html.
8. Excerpt taken from a sermon at www.desiringgod.org/library/topics/gods_passion/god_us_himself.html.
9. Excerpt taken from www.desiringgod.org/library/topics/justification/cb_interview.html.
10. *The Bethlehem Baptist Church Elder Affirmation of Faith* with Scripture proofs can be accessed at www.bbcmpls.org/aboutus/documents/AOFwithESV4-20-04.pdf.
11. Excerpt taken from *Future Grace* (Sisters, Oregon: Multnomah Publishers, 1995), 333.
12. Excerpt taken from www.desiringgod.org/library/tbi/future_grace.html.
13. Excerpt taken from the *Westminster Confession of Faith*, Chapter XI.
14. *Future Grace*, 347.
15. Excerpt taken from www.bbcmpls.org/aboutus/documents/AOFwithESV4-20-04.pdf.
16. *Future Grace*, 101.
17. *Future Grace*, 101.
18. *Future Grace*, 101.
19. *Future Grace*, 112–113.
20. *Future Grace*, 32.

21. *Future Grace*, 48–49.
22. *Future Grace*, 11.
23. *Desiring God*, 112.
24. If you do not own the book, you can find the full text online for free at www.desiringgod.org/dg/id1.htm.
25. *Future Grace*, 115–116.
26. Excerpt taken from *Don't Waste Your Life* (Wheaton, Illinois: Crossway Books, 2003), 96.
27. *Future Grace*, 221.
28. Excerpt taken from www.desiringgod.org/library/topics/money/carnal_cash.html.
29. John Piper's ANTHEM strategies against lust can be found at the *Desiring God* website at the address, http://www.desiringgod.org/library/fresh_words/2001/110501.html.
30. Excerpt taken from www.desiringgod.org/library/sermons/04/092604.html.
31. *Future Grace*, 337–338.
32. *Future Grace*, 261.
33. *Future Grace*, 179.
34. *Future Grace*, 265.
35. 30 minutes is only an approximation. Some of the sessions are shorter, while some are longer. You may need to budget your group time differently, depending upon which session you are viewing.
36. This material has been adapted from curricula produced by The Bethlehem Institute (TBI), a ministry of Bethlehem Baptist Church. It is used by permission.